Mrs. Kelly,
your great!
-♡-Always
Jaclyn Abranams

F

Melissa
Conrey

Dana
Fitchett

Katy Williams

Marsh Avory

Lesley P. bble

Tiffany

Corey Marberry

Nicholas
Carter

Lauren
Thompson

Ryan
Starck

Tommy
CJ Rich

MARY METZGER and
CINTHYA P. WHITTAKER

FOREWORD BY RICHIE HAVENS

A FIRESIDE BOOK PUBLISHED BY SIMON & SCHUSTER

NEW YORK   LONDON   TORONTO   SYDNEY   TOKYO   SINGAPORE

this

planet

TEACHING ENVIRONMENTAL AWARENESS AND APPRECIATION TO CHILDREN

is

mine

Fireside
Simon & Schuster Building
Rockefeller Center
1230 Avenue of the Americas
New York, New York 10020

Copyright © 1991 by Mary Metzger and Cinthya P. Whittaker

FIRESIDE, and colophon are
registered trademarks of Simon & Schuster Inc.

Designed by Bonni Leon

Printed on recycled paper.

Manufactured in the United States of America

10 9 8 7 6 5 4 3 2 1 Pbk.

Library of Congress Cataloging in Publication Data

Metzger, Mary.
This planet is mine : teaching environmental awareness and
appreciation to children / Mary Metzger and Cinthya P. Whittaker :
foreword by Richie Havens.
p. cm.
"A Fireside book."
Includes index.
1. Environmental protection—Citizen participation.
2. Environmental protection—Citizen participation—Study and
teaching. 3. Human ecology. 4. Human ecology—Study and teaching.
I. Whittaker, Cinthya P. II. Title.
TD171.7.M48 1991
372.3'57—dc20
91-18160
CIP

ISBN 0-671-73733-3 Pbk.

ACKNOWLEDGMENTS

**With special thanks
to our friends and families
for their
support and encouragement:**

Carole Dempsey,
for setting her alarm clock
Gwen Edelman
Ron Geatz
Sue Innes, for her gift of time
Betty and Daryl Kan
Kara Leverte
Lisa Novgrod
Bob and Toni Pandini,
grandparents extraordinaire
Our friends at The Nature Conservancy
John Metzger and Jim Whittaker,
for extra dad duty
and Jeff Long . . . always.

For Adam, Eliot, Ian, Lindsey, and Megan

Treat the Earth well.
It was not given to you by your parents.
It was loaned to you by your children.

Kenyan Proverb.

CONTENTS

If we are to understand the delicate balance of Nature's intent for insects, plants, animals, and humans, we must begin to understand that fire, earth, air, and water are the tools with which she works her magic of Natural Balance. And what is Natural Balance? Is it something that existed on Mother Earth long ago but has changed since man came to be born? Were we part of Mother Earth's plan?

These questions were rattling around in my mind before most of my generation began noting changes in the skies and differences in the weather—back when there weren't so many cars, man-made chemicals, and plastics—the days before Styrofoam. In the historical perspective, that time was a mere second ago. Even as a child, I wondered whether these changes were signals, warning us that interference with and a seeming lack of regard for Nature would exact a price.

It seemed to me that if we allowed ourselves to take pleasure in Nature's beauty and majesty without respecting the wisdom of her balance, she would disappear and we would no longer be able to expect the wondrous annual return of the seasons. A time might come when we would say, "The flowers don't grow here anymore," or "The animals have gone . . . forced to do Nature's work elsewhere." Would mankind eventually occupy all the open spaces until they were not the same?

We now know that, planned or not, man has intervened in that delicate balance. Man now occupies many of the Earth's regions that were once shared in harmonious, delicate balance by a variety of species.

Since my early ponderings, I have searched for and learned of ways to work with others to foster respect for Nature. Respect comes first from understanding that there is a problem, and joy comes through learning ways to correct and alter problems by working together to maintain, or regain, that delicate balance.

Sharing that knowledge with the next generation, and harmoniously changing ourselves in the process, offers us pride in the historical future . . . when children will no longer have to worry about the negative possibilities and mistakes we have made.

FOREWORD

Today we are blessed with the concern of many, and enough information to make a difference. We can change problems into learning tools, and energies into working plans and deeds. I have waited a long time for someone to compile enough useful information for the process of public access to begin. Finally it is here, in your hands. This book has within it the potential for creating a new, safe world, and a new potential for human effort to explode in our approach to the new millennium.

If my generation had been offered access to information of this kind, I know for a fact that we would have produced the changes necessary in the human psyche to alter the old ways of thinking about the future and transformed them into a positive approach to living in a safe and prosperous world. In the process, we also would have learned of our importance in Nature's plan—as part of her wonderful, natural dance in the universe.

Richard P. Havens
Chairman of the Board
The Natural Guard

INTRODUCTION

From a great distance the planet Earth looks like a huge ball of swirling blues and greens and whites. The colors mix and mingle, showing us how the land and water meet and touch the cloud-filled skies. This luminous globe is the birthplace of millions of living beings: plants, animals, birds, insects, trees, and people, each with a unique function and purpose, and all dependent upon mutual and harmonious coexistence for survival. From that awesome perspective, all seems well, peaceful, clean. Earth spins gently on her axis, whole and strong, occupied by her eternal journey around the sun. Everything appears to be in its rightful place. But sadly, as we have become increasingly aware, all is not well with planet Earth. Endless numbers of scientists, newspaper headlines, book titles, and political speeches tell us so. They have been telling us for years. But now, with the severity of the tragedy staring at us daily, we are finally beginning to listen.

Gloomy predictions about the failing health of planet Earth have been with us, to one degree or another, for some time. What is different about them in recent years, though, is the growing realization that these predictions, once thought to be the hysterical ramblings of cynics and pessimists, are too quickly becoming reality based on fact and proven experience. They are scientifically founded events that make daily headlines and capture the serious attention not only of their proponents, but of governments, the business community, and individuals from all walks of life as well. According to a recent poll, the number of people concerned about the environment has *doubled* in the last fifteen years. The message is planting itself.

What has aroused all this attention? Imagine this. Scientists predict that by the year 2000:

- Fifty percent of the landfills currently in use in the United States will be closed. (Many of these are currently operating below standard without the proper permits governing standards for health and environmental protection.) Where will we put our trash?

- As much as one-fourth of the Earth's reliable water supply could become unsafe for human use. (Much of this water is already questionable.) What will we drink?
- Seventy percent of the world's rain forests will be lost forever. This is home to hundreds of thousands of species of plants and animals that provide us with food, medicine, and the future of both. How will we measure what we have lost?
- Plants and animals will disappear at the rate of one hundred or more *per day*. If they die, how can we expect to survive much beyond them? How will we feed and clothe ourselves?

These are just a few of the many critically dangerous scenarios we are facing. The bigger picture includes many more. We must now realistically ask ourselves: What are we as human beings doing to ourselves? What will be left of this place for our children and grandchildren?

For years we have demanded that our governments and corporations exercise responsibility for the protection and maintenance of our planet by installing safeguards to prevent environmental damage caused by human activity, and by being prepared to clean up the aftermath of failed safeguards. Intimidated by this huge task, feeling individually helpless and ill-equipped to handle any of the responsibility, we have been content, if not completely comfortable, to leave it in "official" hands. What we are beginning to discover is that our silence and our stillness is more than a little significant. Our complacency is damaging to this Earth, a form of self-destruction with permanent consequences. It desperately needs to be replaced with a more conscientious examination of our daily lives and what each of us is doing individually to disturb the Earth's condition.

Understanding is critical. Action is crucial. When enough people have been exposed to the message, individual action and concern will translate into collective action and concern. The Earth's condition is serious—but together, by acting in unison as individuals, we can help it recover to a reasonable degree. This is our home, a home we share and on which we depend, along with a multitude of other living beings, for survival.

To act, we must first understand the issues, learn what effect our daily lives have on the environment, then find ways to lessen our impact. The mission of this book is to ensure the success of this knowledge and its daily application—to ensure that it lasts longer than our own lifetimes. How? The question can be answered in one brief imperative: Share the knowledge with your children. Teach them what you know. Build their lives on the fundamentals of respect for and nurturing of their planet. After all, we will pass it into their hands, just as the previous generation passed it into ours.

Demonstrate by action how to assume responsibility, and explain why it is so vital. Each chapter provides basic information on the critical issues facing the Earth and their relative importance to the survival of all species. Use these as your guidelines when presenting the information to your children. Don't worry that this information may be too advanced for the younger age groups. It can be tailored to suit your needs and the comprehension level of the children you are presenting it to. You'll be surprised at their readiness and willingness to participate in this learning process.

Our discussion of each critical issue is followed by ways in which you and your children can make a difference in that area—through changes in the way you live. The daily lifestyle choices you make can help the healing process of the planet. You will find some overlap as you read through the chapters. This is inevitable because of the interdependence of the Earth's various natural processes. For example, you may read about recycling or water issues in several chapters. Doing so will help you understand the connections that exist between all living things and the natural world.

Also included are learning activities in which everyone can participate—experiments and projects that inform as well as nurture a broader understanding of the interconnectedness of all of nature's beings and the natural processes we all share. Try to link these activities with current events, or your child's particular concerns.

We'll tell you about books you can read and organizations you can join that will help you even further. Included as one of the several informational appendices is a glossary to help you make sense of the jargon and terminology of the environmental movement.

This book provides a number of different alternatives to many of its offerings. Not all of them may be right for you or your children. Do what you can. Participation, no matter how minor, is a step in the right direction. Involving your children, no matter how little, is the key.

In some instances there will be little that they can actually do themselves, but they can be taught about *your* actions and why you choose to engage in boycotting, for example, or only buy products from environmentally responsible companies. If we don't take the time to share information with them now, the critical lessons we are learning will be lost. There will be no time to teach them to the next generation in the next decade. It will require forethought on your part. Take your time. Be patient. Explain. Prepare them.

We have a responsibility to preserve and protect not just one another, but all those with whom we share the air, water, and land. The diversity of life—each plant and animal, and the places they need to survive—plays a part in the life pattern. Each is useful. Each is interconnected and interdependent on others because it uses or is used by, nourishes or is nourished by, them. The maintenance of this pattern is what keeps the Earth healthy and balanced. Any disruption of that diversity upsets the balance.

When you're not actively engaged in the day-to-day work of cleaning up the planet, use your political and consumer voices to effect change in the policies of others. Politicians, manufacturers, and service providers will listen when you withhold your vote, or your money.

Use your conviction, your commitment, and these pages to guide you through. Your positive action will prove to be one of the best legacies you leave to your children, for it will encourage them to follow your lead as they grow into adulthood.

Remember, this planet is yours—this planet is theirs—this planet is mine.

this
planet
is
mine

air

Through woods and mountain passes
The winds like anthems roll.

Henry Wadsworth Longfellow

AIR is the mixture of gases—mostly oxygen and nitrogen (along with hydrogen, carbon dioxide, argon, helium, and more)—that surrounds the Earth. This layer of gases, called the atmosphere, is approximately 310 miles thick and acts as a protective screen by keeping the fierce rays of the sun from burning up the planet. The oxygen in air is what we need to breathe to purify our blood and keep our hearts pumping—a rather critical aspect of all animal life.

We cannot see air (or shouldn't be able to, pollutants can often make air visible), but we can feel it when the wind and breezes blow. It is a constant reminder of one of life's most critical sustaining forces, a soothing touch when it blows gently, an angry power when it gathers in a storm.

Many of the world's critical environmental issues are connected in one way or another to air: ozone depletion, global warming, acid rain, and even human illness.

issue

Any toxic gases or fine particles that enter the air pose a threat to our health because we inhale anything that floats along with the oxygen. They can be responsible for genetic defects, respiratory ailments, cancer, and contribute to heart and lung diseases as well. Many unseen airborne toxins are also critically damaging lakes, streams, forests, crops, soil, and even buildings. Certain pollutants like chlorofluorocarbons (CFCs), which are emitted into the air from the use of aerosol sprays, refrigerants, and Styrofoam products (among other things), are seriously damaging the Earth's protective ozone layer. We've all heard about the "hole in the ozone layer" that threatens to allow dangerous ultraviolet sun rays to penetrate the atmosphere.

Burning fossil fuels to propel our cars, buses, and airplanes, as well as to facilitate certain industrial practices, increases the amount of carbon dioxide, a heat-absorbing gas, in the atmosphere. The resulting "global warming" is already being accused of altering weather patterns, agricultural output, and more.

Because we can't *see* these distortions occurring, we tend to view our contribution to the problem in a less than serious light. But the problems are here and they are growing at an alarming rate. We are contributing to them.

OUTDOOR AIR POLLUTION:
THE MAJOR OFFENDERS

Considering that the Earth is billions of years old, air pollution is a relatively new problem for our planet. The earliest offenders date back to the industrial revolution when air-polluting, coal-fueled factories set the stage for what has now evolved into the vast array of toxic substances that we spew into our atmosphere.

Societies worldwide have based their growth-structure on the very offenders that cause the problem. Our transportation, industrial, and energy systems are all based on globally devastating air-polluting technologies which pump billions of tons of pollutants into the atmosphere each year. A great deal of damage has already been done, forcing us to confront the issue. In fact, many major urban area newspapers now add a description of daily air pollution levels along with their weather reports. Winning the battle against this problem will require drastic, soul-searching change. New technologies cannot undo the problem or make it go away, they can only help us to cope and preserve what's left.

Our Transportation System

As adults, our main contribution to air pollution sits in our garage or driveway. Automobiles are a primary source of the air pollution that is often referred to now as the "ground-level ozone problem." Our cars emit many toxic substances, including large amounts of carbon monoxide, which interfere with the blood's ability to absorb oxygen, which in turn may threaten the growth and mental development of unborn babies. Other automotive by-products include: lead, which affects the circulatory, reproductive, kidney, and nervous systems and is suspected of causing hyperactivity and learning disabilities in children; nitrogen dioxide, which increases our susceptibility to viral infections; ozone, which irritates our respiratory system; and toxic emissions, which serve as a "catchall" category that includes chemical compounds known to cause cancer, reproductive problems, and birth defects. The crisis won't go away in this generation. Improving it is doubtful, unless we make a strong commitment to driving less and using much more fuel-efficient cars.

make a difference!

▶ 1 Riding a bicycle is the cleanest and most efficient means of transportation. Make an effort to ride a bike whenever possible. Consider using your bike or walking for short errands. How many of us hop in the car for a simple trip to the corner store for a loaf of bread? One hundred miles' worth of short car rides spews more pollutants into the air than a straight, hundred-mile car trip because the catalytic converter in your automobile does not control pollution until it is warmed up. That can take about five minutes.

- Bike ride together. Bicycle carts are available that can accommodate two children and a couple of bags of groceries.
- Encourage bicycle safety skills at an early age and enjoy the time together.

▶ 2 If you cannot walk or bike, opt for a car pool, or use public transportation. Your children have probably been part of some type of car pool already.

- Carpooling information is often available in the Yellow Pages of your telephone book.
- Advertise your desire to carpool at your place of business. It's usually quite easy to find a few people who live reason-

ably close to one another and appreciate the shared ex-
penses.

▶ **3** Work at home if it's possible.

▶ **4** When shopping for a new car, take interested children with
you and explain what you are looking for and why. Consider:

- Choosing an energy-efficient model, which gets at least 45
  miles to the gallon.
- Avoiding car air conditioners. Automobile air conditioners
  emit CFCs (Freon) into the atmosphere. If you do choose
  air-conditioning for your new car, make an effort to have it
  serviced regularly at a reliable garage that recycles the
  CFCs, and have them recycled out of your old car before it is
  scrapped.
- Choosing a light color with tinted glass. The light color of
  the car will help to reflect the sun's heat, and the tinted
  glass will help keep the sun's glare to a minimum, reducing
  your need for air-conditioning.
- Looking for good radial tires with a high tread rating. The
  technology for lifetime tires exists, but it will be several
  years before we see them—many tire companies would
  go out of business if the product was made readily available.
- Doing your homework before shopping for that new car.
  Check records at your local library or pick up some consumer magazines. Look for maintenance records, crash
  tests, safety features, energy efficiency, and reliability. It
  has been suggested that if everyone in the United States
  drove a car with a minimum fuel efficiency of 45 miles per
  gallon, we would not need to subsidize our domestic oil supplies with foreign oil. It's an interesting proposition, given
  our country's involvement in the Middle East.

▶ **5** Drive with an environmental consciousness. Keeping your car
in good condition reduces the amount of fuel consumed and the
amount of toxic emissions released into the atmosphere. It also sets
a good example for the future drivers in the family.

- Avoid using your air-conditioning. One charge of Freon from
  an auto air conditioner is estimated to contribute as much to
  global warming as the carbon dioxide emitted from an average new car driven 20,000 miles.

- Have your car exhaust emission levels checked annually and make any necessary repairs. Something as simple as a tune-up can make your engine operate more efficiently and reduce harmful emissions. Tune-ups are recommended every 5,000 miles.
- Avoid high-octane gasoline unless it is required for the efficient operation of your car.
- Keep your car tires properly inflated. Check them once a week or every time you "fill up."
- Consolidate errands into one trip.
- Avoid long warm-ups, accelerate gently, and adhere to the speed limit.
- If possible, avoid the rush-hour traffic. Prolonged idling of your car while waiting in traffic or "drive-thru" lines can use up gas at the rate of one-half gallon per hour.
- Recycle used motor oil and batteries.
- Remove heavy objects from your car. The lighter the car, the less fuel it will burn.

▶ **6** Convince your senators and representatives of the need for more energy-efficient automobiles. Communicate your concern about the air pollution problem. (See Effective Letter Writing in Appendix 3.)

Our Industrial Technologies

Since the dawning of the industrial revolution, when profits became the priority, industry has been slow to achieve an acceptable level of environmental consciousness. The global industrial complex dumps millions of tons of pollutant waste into the air each day. CFCs are only one small example of industrial abuse. CFCs are the man-made, primary greenhouse gases causing depletion of the outer layer of our atmosphere. Created less than one hundred years ago, they are still being produced despite their known contribution to human and environmental degradation. Reoutfitting and retooling industry to become more responsible is an expensive proposition, and, as we know, for industry, profits are always the bottom line. But as parents and consumers we must make *environmental responsibility* the bottom line, and choose to spend our money on Earth-saving, not Earth-destroying products and technologies.

Our Energy Consumption

It's difficult to consciously accept the fact that when we use gas and electricity in our homes, we're polluting our air. But the fact remains that over 85 percent of electrical power around the world is supplied by fossil fuels including gas, oil, and coal. Nuclear power supplies the rest, and its destructive power is well known. Burning fossil fuels is a primary cause of air pollution. By becoming more energy efficient you can make a difference. For example, by simply investing in alternative energy-efficient light bulbs you can keep thousands of tons of carbon dioxide out of the atmosphere each year. The more efficient your use of energy at home, the less stress there is on hydroelectric power plants, which emit millions of tons of carbon dioxide into the air yearly.

Waste Management

Although incineration is promoted today as "waste to energy" or "resource recovery," in reality it continues to be a source of serious air pollution and undermines efforts to recycle, which experts agree is ultimately a basic concept crucial to our planet's survival. Incinerators burn all products, including many toxic substances, without discretion. It is estimated that for every ton of incinerated material, 30 percent of the result is toxic ash. The impact upon vegetation and water is yet to be determined. The known consequences to the ever-growing pressure to incinerate community waste include the multiple health risks associated with the absorption of pollutants through the skin, and their bioaccumulation in our food chain. In essence, the toxic substances we burn today will not go away. They will build up in our body tissue and cause diseases such as cancer.

Do you know if there's an incinerator used or planned for use in your community? Most citizens do not know. Yet our health and that of our families is at stake. Choosing to promote, practice, and vote for recycling projects is a viable alternative to incineration.

THE GLOBAL EFFECTS

In order to grasp the enormity of the effect air pollution has on the planet, we must first understand the "atmospheric balance" of the air surrounding the Earth. The planet is surrounded by various layers of gases. These layered blankets of protective gases keep the ultraviolet sun rays (UV radiation) at bay, enabling life to exist and flourish. Any imbalance in this protective layer causes an inordinate number of harmful rays to penetrate the atmosphere and become trapped.

Atmospheric balance is achieved when 80 percent nitrogen, 20 percent oxygen, and trace amounts of other gases form the protective layer. Air pollution is upsetting this balance. Carbon dioxide (an atmospheric gas) is appearing as a much larger percentage of the atmosphere as a result of our dependence on burning fossil fuels for energy. It is estimated that carbon dioxide, because of its heat-absorbing properties, accounts for approximately one-half of the global warming trend.

Another by-product of fossil fuel combustion reaching excessive levels is nitrous oxide. Deforestation, the breakdown of widely used nitrogen fertilizers, and the growth in ground-level ozone smog all contribute to its formation.

Methane, a by-product of the bacterial decomposition of organic matter, is yet another atmospheric gas growing in relative percentage. Rice paddies, swamps, landfills, and livestock flatulence all create methane. Its atmospheric proportions are believed to be increasing because more livestock is being bred and more rice cultivated to feed our ever-increasing global population.

Other gases present in smaller percentages in the air include water vapor and man-made CFCs. But even these "greenhouse gases" are growing in volume, and affect the entire world.

Global Warming

As the sun radiates and warms the planet, there is a certain amount of heat that is not absorbed by land or water. This heat radiates back into space as infrared energy. Today, more and more of this infrared heat is being trapped in the Earth's atmosphere because of the growing percentage of "greenhouse gases" (or heat-absorbing gases). The effect on our planet is analogous to the glass walls and roof of a greenhouse that hold in the sun-warmed air. This same process is occurring on Earth, hence the term "greenhouse effect."

Scientists can now measure this heating-up of our planet. As

they project their findings into the next fifty years the consequences appear grim, to say the least. Although temperatures will
become warmer, they will not be evenly distributed around the
globe. Winters will become warmer and summers hotter in many
parts of the world. Yet temperatures around the equator will
hardly change. Areas of high rainfall will have even higher precipitation levels. Areas of light rainfall will become barren deserts.
Global warming will cause the partial meltdown of Arctic and
alpine glaciers, creating a rise in sea level. Many of the world's
major cities, and nearly half of their populations, live in areas
where a rise in sea level will have devastating consequences. Wet-
land ecosystems will be destroyed and drinking water supplies will
be contaminated by salt water.

Natural disasters such as "superhurricanes" will become increasingly common. As temperatures increase, the vicious cycle of
abuse will increase as more people respond by using more fossil
fuels to "'air-condition" themselves in comfort. There will be more
droughts and fires, and rapid warming will ravage many species of
plant and animal life.

At this point in time, the issue is not whether global warming
will cause disaster, but *how quickly* this disaster will occur. Global
warming is at the forefront of international environmental concerns, but one factor scientists cannot predict is how fast the devastation will occur. We must make every effort to slow down the
warming process by reducing the amount of "greenhouse gases"
that are pumped into the atmosphere. We have no other choice.

Ozone Depletion

The outer layer of the Earth's atmosphere, the stratosphere, is
responsible for screening out much of the sun's harmful ultraviolet
radiation. This thin layer of air, the ozone layer, is deteriorating,
and holes have been found in it in recent years.

How did this happen? Short-sighted ignorance is the answer. As
eager chemists were searching for new compounds that would
somehow "enhance" our lives, they, along with industry, failed to
consider the environmental impact their man-made products
would have. Profits, as always, overruled common sense, and the
world is only now beginning to study and understand the results.

Chlorofluorocarbons, one form of industrial waste, are now

known to cause ozone depletion. CFCs are extremely efficient at breaking down the oxygen molecules which make up the ozone layer. The breakdown creates a hole that allows harmful UV radiation to filter through to the planet's surface. UV radiation has already been revealed as a contributing factor in DNA-damage and resultant genetic defects. It has caused damage to crops, fish eggs, and phytoplankton, microscopic plant life which is an essential link in the food chain that determines the survival of numerous fish species. Ultraviolet rays also contribute to the dramatic increase we have seen in skin cancers, eye cataracts, and associated eye problems, and impair the human immune system, reducing our ability to fight disease.

It has been suggested that even if the entire world were immediately to stop using products containing CFCs, the destruction of the ozone layer would go on for decades. The reason for this grim forecast is that CFC molecules take twenty to fifty years to reach the ozone layer, and then remain in the atmosphere for as long as three hundred years. In other words, the aerosol spray or Styrofoam ice chest that you use today will cause further destruction well into your grandchildren's generation. Recovery will take more than a century.

Other known ozone-depleting chemicals include halons, carbon tetrachloride, hydrochlorofluorocarbons (HCFCs), and methyl chloride. Many man-made chemical compounds are being created every day to supposedly enhance and simplify our lives, and the list of ozone-depleting chemicals is sure to increase as scientists continue to study the problem. As a global concern, it is clear that we've already done too little, too late. Regulations for the use of CFCs have been discussed, but these chemicals will still be produced for another ten years and maybe longer in less developed countries.

Ozone Smog

It's important to understand the difference between ozone depletion and ground-level ozone. The two problems are often confused and one mistaken for the other. Ozone, or O_3, is an essential layer of protection in our outer atmosphere. At ground level it is destructive and unwelcome smog.

Ozone smog, a major greenhouse gas, is formed when car exhaust and other emissions combine and react with sunlight. The result is smog—air pollution we can often see and smell. In high concentrations it gives us headaches and reduces lung efficiency. There's no escaping ozone smog. Until we start using cleaner, more efficient sources of transportation, and reduce what we use now, ozone smog will remain.

make a difference!

▶ Avoid using products containing CFCs. The following list of violators may surprise you. The list includes products that contain CFCs and/or those products which use CFCs in their manufacture.

Automobile air conditioners
Automobile dashboards, door padding, and seat cushions
Bicycle seats
Bronchial-inhalant medications
Calculators
Cameras
Carpet pads
Chewing-gum remover
Clothes dryers
Clothes washing machines
Computer and camera dusters
Computer disk envelopes
Contact lenses
Dishwashers
Dry-cleaning fluids
Electronic toys
Express mail envelopes
Foam drinking cups
Foam ice chests
Foam packing chips
Foam pillows and mattresses
Freezer insulation
Furniture cushions
Heat pumps
Home air conditioners

Home freezers
Ice cream and yogurt machines
Ice machines
Jewelry (some)
Lenses for glasses
Low-tar tobacco
Microwave ovens
Photocopiers
Portable fire extinguishers
Postal mailers
Radios
Roof insulation
Silly string toys
Smoke alarms
Solvents
Spices (some)
Sports cushions
Styro-type egg cartons
Supermarket meat trays
Telephones
Televisions
Toy stuffing
Typewriters
Urethane-soled shoes
VCRs
Vending machines

Acid Rain

Acid rain is produced when fossil fuels are burned by cars, power plants, and industry. Millions of tons of sulphur dioxide and nitrogen oxide are blown into the atmosphere where they mix with the water that eventually becomes snow and rain. Once the contact with water is made, oxides are converted into nitric and sulphuric acids. The two acids are suspended in the atmosphere for a long time, but eventually fall to Earth in the form of harmful acid precipitation that literally kills rivers, lakes, trees, and agricultural crops.

This deadly precipitation is also capable of damaging many manmade structures. Limestone and marble buildings, bridges, historical monuments, gravestones, and statues become pitted, weakened, and defaced by acid rain.

In addition, when acid rain hits the ground it dissolves valuable minerals in the soil and carries them away. It burns leaves, slows plant growth, and changes the chemical characteristics of streams and lakes, threatening ecosystems by limiting food supplies for fish and even preventing their eggs from hatching.

In terms of our own health, acid rain has some serious detrimental effects.

- There is a strong connection between acid rain and increased incidences of lung ailments, especially asthma, in children.
- When it enters the water supply, acid rain can leach out harmful metals, especially those in the lead pipes that are often used to conduct your drinking water.
- High levels of mercury are found in some acid lakes, affecting fish which are consumed by humans. The potential health risks are enormous.

Acid rain is a threat of global proportions. It crosses borders and invades our wildlands and communities with little to hinder it. It invades countries that have little or no industrial base on which to lay the blame. It is as frightening a problem as all the others which affect our air quality, and one that clearly reflects the adverse effect our modernization has had on the planet. We have created a global greenhouse which, if not dealt with, will pass into the lives of our children with such irreversible magnitude that no remedy will be powerful enough.

It is a crisis, and one that requires our individual attention if we are to find a solution.

make a difference!

▶ **1** Conserve energy in your home.

- Call your utility company and ask for an energy audit. They will help you pinpoint ways to improve energy efficiency and teach you how to conserve.

- Set your thermostat at reasonable temperatures, keeping them a little cooler in the winter and a little warmer in the summer.

Consider installing a thermostat with a timer that turns the heat off when you're asleep at night and turns it back on an hour before you wake up.

Wear warmer clothing around the house in the winter and cooler clothing in the summer.

Take steps to insulate your home with weather stripping, caulking, window insulation, and general insulation.

Seal and do not heat unused rooms.

Close fireplace dampers when not in use. Warm air stays in, cold air stays out.

Avoid using air-conditioning.

- It is worth paying a higher price for energy-efficient appliances. You'll notice a satisfying difference when you pay a lower monthly utility bill.

When possible, opt for natural gas appliances as opposed to electric.

To find out about efficient appliances, contact:

The Association of Home Appliance Manufacturers
20 N. Wacker Dr.
Chicago, IL 60606

Gas Appliance Manufacturers Association.
1901 N. Fort Myer Dr.
Arlington, VA 22209

• Wash your laundry in cold water. Up to 90 percent of the energy used to wash clothes is used to heat the water.
• Dry your clothes outside whenever possible.

Clothes can be given a quick "ironing" by hanging them in the bathroom while you shower. It will save having to turn on the iron, and a little time for you as well.

• Keep your freezer and refrigerator full, allowing enough space for air to circulate.

Conserve energy by making fewer trips to the fridge and by keeping the door open for only a few seconds.
Set the temperature at the lowest reasonable setting.
Install a solar refrigerator. For more information, contact:

Alternative Energy Engineering, Inc.
P.O. Box 339
Redway, CA 95560

• When an incandescent light bulb goes, consider a long-life bulb as a replacement. Compact fluorescent light bulbs are now available that use one-fourth the energy and last for years. They have a higher purchase price but the savings in energy and replacement cost make them the most economical choice.

▶ 2 Invest your money in Earth-conscious, alternative technologies. Support research in solar, biomass (organic) fuels, and wind energy. These are cleaner sources of energy, much kinder to the planet, and they promote energy independence.

▶ 3 Consider using hand-operated instead of machine-operated equipment and appliances whenever possible. Electric can openers and electric knives are no more effective than a little "elbow grease."

▶ **4** On a local level, become active on the city council, parent-teacher association, school board, chamber of commerce, or in a local environmental group. You can even do-it-yourself and start a local tree-planting project in your community, lobby for bicycle lanes, or suggest to the utility company that they include energy- and water-saving information with the monthly bill. Volunteering and speaking out are the positive beginnings of change.

▶ **5** Plant trees together. Growing trees from seed can be a wonderful family project. As children grow so will the trees. Not only are they sentimental reminders, they store carbon dioxide and fight global warming. Try to plant at least one tree per year as your family effort to fight global warming.

▶ **6** Give trees as gifts. For $1.00 you can get one tree from the:

National Arbor Day Foundation
100 Arbor Ave.
Nebraska City, NE 68410
402-474-5655

Many other environmental organizations have tree-planting programs that will plant a tree in the name of a friend or loved one as a gift.

▶ **7** Buy and wear clothes that are made of natural fibers, washable fabrics, and clothes that are not shipped from the far ends of the Earth, wasting energy for transport. Avoid clothing that requires dry cleaning. Dry-cleaning solvents release CFCs. Hang your clothes to "air" if they are not soiled and do not require cleaning.

learning activities

▶ **1** Create an energy plan and see if your home, school, or office measures up to the following guidelines. Have the kids follow you around with a clipboard listing these points and let them be a part of the process.

- Start by asking what forms of energy are currently being used. Talk about fossil fuels: where they come from, how they'll run out, and what we can do to save energy at home. For instance, fossil fuels are made up of the remains of ancient plants and animals (dinosaurs) which eventually turn into coal, oil, and natural gas deep below the Earth's surface. Burning fossil fuels in our homes, cars, and factories has created air pollution. You can then make the point that we can reduce the amount of fossil fuels we burn which, in turn, will reduce air pollution.

• Check for drafts around the windows and doors. Do you have storm windows or double-paned windows for the winter months? Learn to draw curtains to keep down the draft on very cold days and the sun out on very warm days. Talk about ways you can keep the heat in during the cold months and lock the heat out in the summer.

• Are the doors kept closed to rooms that are not in use? Heat and air-conditioning vents can be adjusted or closed completely in these rooms to save energy.

• Is the water heater insulated with a thermal blanket? What's the setting on the water heater? It should be below 120 degrees F.

• Is the chimney damper closed when not in use? Warm air can easily escape through the chimney, wasting energy.

• Have you made the transition to energy-efficient light bulbs?

• Do you avoid using the "Auto Dry" setting on the dishwasher and simply prop the door open so the dishes can drip-dry? This habit can save energy. Make sure both the dishwasher and washing machine are full before you start the load. Why not just wash and dry dishes the old-fashioned way—by hand?

• Do you have a clothesline or drying rack to use when the weather's right for air drying your clothes?

• Are any unnecessary lights, radios, or televisions turned off?

• Do you have faucet and shower aerators to reduce the amount of hot water flow, ultimately saving both water and energy?

• Think of more things to add to your checklist and pass it around. Use a point system to see how your scores compare.

• Do you use any alternate forms of energy? Solar or wind power?

▶ **2** Make bumper stickers: "Save our planet and save lives," "Drive 55 MPH," or "We recycle, do you?" Be creative.

▶ **3** Talk about the sun and its effect on us.

- Talk about hot and cold colors. Explain how some colors reflect heat while others absorb it.
- Discuss how harmful UV rays of the sun cannot be seen. Choose some materials from around the house, including various pieces of scrap paper (black, green, red), colored glass or a prism, clear glass or a magnifying glass, a mirror or some foil. If you have any thermometers, shake them down to the same temperature and use those, too. Sit near a window and hold the different items up to the light. Talk about how some things block light while others absorb it, and how a mirror or foil will reflect light and something opaque or crystal will divide the rays.
- Put a pinhole in a piece of paper and see how the rays shine through. With older children this may open up discussion about the ozone hole.
- Lay thermometers on different pieces of colored paper and record the different temperatures after ten minutes. You can decide what colors to wear on a warm day to reflect the sun's heat and what colors to wear when you want to stay warm. The directions this activity can take are endless depending on the different ages of the children.

▶ **4** Try to "catch" pollution. Using some cellophane tape or a thin layer of lip balm spread on scraps of cardboard you can document the air pollution problem around your home or school.

- Put the cards with the tape (sticky side up) in different locations; for example, near the road, in a tree, and indoors.
- Check the cards a day or two later for a visual record of the air pollution you've collected. If pollution is present, there will be particles on the tape and it will be a darker color. You may want to use these cards as proof of the problem when you approach the school or city about your concerns.

▶ **5** Discuss the movement of wind. Use the following activities to show your child the power of the air. Try them inside and outside, even on a windy day, while discussing the value of wind power as an alternate source of energy.

• Make pinwheels together and talk about how air moves even though you can't see it. Open up the discussion to include wind power and energy. You'll need:

a square piece of paper
a straw
a paper fastener
scissors

Make diagonal cuts on each of the four corners of the paper toward the center. (Leave plenty of room to insert the fastener.)

Pull one corner of each of the "triangles" formed toward the center.

Make a small incision and insert the fastener through each of the gathered corners.

Insert the pinwheel through one end of the straw and fasten it at the back. It's as simple as that.

If your children are interested in decorating the pinwheel, it should be done before the paper is cut and fastened to the straw.

• Make a mobile together. Suspend it from the ceiling and watch how it moves in even the slightest currents of air. Many hobby stores sell kits to make your mobile. This may be a good idea for novices, since it is sometimes difficult to achieve the necessary balance if you are not familiar with the physics of mobile construction.
• Make paper airplanes. (If you've forgotten how, you can buy one.) Fly the plane inside and out. Measure distances and discuss how the air moves. Consider this a lesson in aerodynamics and try to build a more energy-efficient paper airplane that flies further.
• Fly a kite!
• Blow bubbles, or make giant bubbles together. You'll need:

¾ cup Karo corn syrup
2 cups Joy dishwashing liquid

6 cups water
a coat hanger

Mix the liquid ingredients in a shallow pan.
Bend the hanger into a smooth, round shape.
Swish the hanger around in the pan and point it in the direction of the wind. The moving air will help force the soapy mixture through the hanger. You'll create beautiful giant bubbles.
Discuss how this is a visual confirmation of the strength and the directional movement of air. What happens if you hold the bubble wand away from the wind? Do bubbles emerge?

▶ **6** Hang laundry together on the clothesline and talk about the heat of the sun. While you're doing it, stretch a rubber band between two clothespins on the line. Check the rubber band in a few days, a week, and a couple of weeks if it lasts. If it deteriorates quickly you may live in an area with poor air quality. You can talk more about the air pollution in your neighborhood and what can be done about it.

▶ **7** Make an effort to learn how to read your gas or electric meter at home and then teach the children. It will be interesting for them (and you!) to see how much energy is used on any given day.

- Do an experiment to test the usage on a weekday when everyone is at school and work, and on a weekend day when there is much more activity around the house. Check it once in the morning before everyone becomes too active, and again at night just before everyone goes to bed.
- See what happens if you make an effort to keep certain appliances off. How is the usage affected?

▶ **8** To understand what will happen to the oceans in the event of global warming, try this simple experiment.

Fill a glass with water and place it in the sun.
Add a couple of ice cubes to the glass—as if icebergs have broken from land and are to melt in the ocean. Does the water level in the glass rise as these mini-icebergs are

added? Imagine if the world's oceans became filled with icebergs from melting glaciers due to global warming.

INDOOR AIR POLLUTION:
A HIDDEN HAZARD

Today, the level of toxic air pollutants inside most homes is higher than that of the air outside. The toxicity of indoor air is often as much as *ten times* the level of outdoor air pollution, and well above the maximum allowable outdoor standards established by the government. This is inside our homes, where we eat, sleep, and spend time with our friends and family! Why is this happening?

As we have become more energy efficient, there has been a significant decrease in the ventilation in our homes, office buildings, stores, shopping malls, schools—just about any modern indoor environment. Windows are kept closed or, as is the case with many modern office buildings, cannot be opened at all. The standard building supplies used in construction and remodeling—such as synthetic materials, plastics, gas appliances, scented items, cleaning products, pesticides, and paneling—generally have a higher noxious fume content than many harmful outdoor pollutants. Trapped within the buildings and capable of being released at various times, they are a continuing hazard. Other indoor pollutants include tobacco smoke, dust, mold, and radon, an invisible, odorless gas that is released when uranium-laced soil and rock decay into radioactive particles.

To add to the problem, each home is different, with a variety of potentially harmful gases or combinations of pollutants that may have even graver consequences. The synergistic effects—the joint action of two substances having a much greater effect than a single substance—of many indoor pollutants are virtually unknown.

Radon Gas

A particularly dangerous synergistic combination of indoor pollutants is radon and tobacco smoke. The combined effects of these two pollutants are considerably higher than the sum of their individual effects. A family living in a home in which these two toxins combine and interact on a regular basis puts itself "invisibly" in serious jeopardy of developing lung or other cancers.

Radon levels can vary from day to day depending on atmospheric pressure, the moisture content of the soil, and changes in ventilation. Unless the house is tested, there may be a veritable time bomb ticking away, unsuspected until some point in the future when a family member develops a serious illness and a cause is sought.

There are steps you can take to protect your family if you suspect high radon levels in your area. Generally beware of basements with dirt floors, since radon gas rises through porous soil. Recent studies indicate that there are twelve states with elevated radon levels: Connecticut, Colorado, Florida, Kentucky, Maine, New Hampshire, New Jersey, New York, Ohio, Pennsylvania, Tennessee, and Utah. Contact your state health department regarding radon levels in your community.

▶ **1** Have your home tested over a three- or four-day period during the summer and winter. This is important because levels can fluctuate considerably during seasonal changes. Because radon originates in the soil and rock under your home, the test should be conducted at the lowest level of the house, preferably in the basement. Do-it-yourself kits are not always reliable, and it is better to use the service of an EPA-approved laboratory.

▶ **2** Stop smoking and keep others from smoking inside your house, especially if radon is suspected; this will halt the synergistic effects of tobacco smoke and radon.

▶ **3** Follow the guidelines for protecting your home and correcting defects if radon is found. The best source of information for all radon inquiries and information is the:

Environmental Protection Agency
Office of Radiation Programs
820 Quincy St., N.W.
Washington, D.C. 20011

Who's at Risk?

Those who spend a considerable amount of time indoors, including children and the elderly, are particularly at risk of developing reactions to indoor air pollution. Children breathe faster than adults and as a result breathe in more air pollution per pound of body weight. Since a small child's immune system is not fully developed until about ten years of age, hypersensitivity to pollutants may develop. The elderly are at risk as well because their immune systems are often declining and thus are more susceptible to the effects of chemical hypersensitivity. But as the ozone is depleted in our atmosphere, and ultraviolet rays begin to affect our immune systems, we will *all* be faced with potential immune system inefficiency. Indoor pollution will then become much more of an issue.

A small but growing percentage of our population is already developing what the medical profession calls "Chemical Hypersensitivity Syndrome" (CHS). People who develop Chemical Hypersensitivity Syndrome exhibit reactions to extremely small amounts of pollution. This easily triggered condition may be the result of heavy exposure to the offending chemicals at an early age. It makes sense then to eliminate these chemicals from your home immediately. We can all benefit, and possibly even see minor, less critical chronic health problems—allergies, for example—disappear as we clean up our indoor air.

Clinical ecologists, those doctors who specialize in the treatment of Chemical Hypersensitivity Syndrome, agree that the most important thing we can do to improve our health and guard against the development of CHS is to identify and avoid the chemicals that cause the problem. Two nonprofit support groups have formed to help answer the questions and concerns you may have about this condition.

Human Ecology Action League (HEAL)
P.O. Box 66637
Chicago, IL 60666
312-665-6575

National Foundation for the Chemically Hypersensitive
P.O. Box 9
Wrightsville Beach, NC 28480
919-256-5391

One other kind of indoor pollution, which we tend to forget is a form of pollution at all, is noise. Indoor noise seems unavoidable, but many forms of noise pollution need not be taken for granted. Not only are our children noisy, indoor technology is noisy as well. Refrigerators hum, clocks tick, phones ring, televisions blare, vacuum cleaners roar, and on and on. Noise pollution seems to be a by-product of our technological advances. Scientists agree that even normal noise levels can create stress in our bodies. Added stress is a hazard that adults and children don't need in their lives. Consider noise levels when shopping for a new home. Choosing a home on a heavily traveled street or backing up on the local community swimming pool may not be in your best interest.

make a difference!

▶ 1 Ventilate your home and office. There are a couple of products available on the market to help:

- Air-to-air heat exchangers. These units, which can be installed either in windows or as part of the central air system, ventilate by drawing outside air indoors, and conserve energy by retrieving heat that is directed outdoors.
- Air cleaners, or air purifiers. These devices range from small tabletop units (good for office use) to central air systems. Though they are seldom strong enough to collect gases from the air, they can be effective at removing small, airborne particles of dust, etc. New ventilation systems are being developed and many building contractors are becoming educated on improved ventilation techniques and products. When remodeling or building a new home do your homework before hiring a contractor.

▶ 2 Consider having your air ducts, filters, and heating and air-conditioning units professionally cleaned of excess dirt and dust.

▶ 3 If you have an attached garage, try to avoid using it to store your car—toxic buildups will occur from your car's exhaust system.

▶ 4 Spend more time outdoors. If you live in an urban area, take yourself off to the country, away from freeways and industrial sites, for a little "fresh air."

▶ **5** Reduce your domestic contribution to the problem. Avoid as many toxic products as possible. These include:

* Most household cleaning products. Try using environmentally safe products or simple, natural alternatives like baking soda, salt, white vinegar, lemon juice, Borax, and nonchlorinated scouring powder.

* Avoid highly toxic drain cleaners, oven cleaners, ammonia- and chlorox-based cleansers, furniture and floor polishes, metal cleaners, mold and mildew cleaners, disinfectants, carpet shampoos, dishwasher detergents, glass cleaners, air fresheners, household pesticides, perfumes and scented products including hair sprays and mothballs, many art supplies and paint, formaldehyde-based paneling, synthetic carpets, gas and kerosene appliances, spot removers, dry-cleaning chemicals, fabric softeners, spray starches, and laundry detergents.

▶ **6** Choose furniture and food containers that are not made with CFC foam. It's become quite common to market and advertise products as having "No CFCs." If you don't know whether the product contains CFCs, but suspect that it does, don't buy it.

▶ **7** Avoid halon fire extinguishers, as they emit a greenhouse gas (halon), and choose smoke detectors that do not use radioactive materials. The safe home fire extinguisher is a dry chemical type which uses sodium bicarbonate as the extinguishing agent.

learning activities

▶ **1** Make an effort to reduce the level of noise in your home: unplug loud appliances, turn off the television and radio when no one is watching or listening, and send the kids outside when they absolutely must play Cowboys and Indians. To help you realize the varieties and levels of noise you endure in your daily life try this little experiment.

* Sit quietly with your child and listen to the sounds in your house. Don't make an effort to eliminate any of the noises before you do this. Help your child discern the various noises and make a list. How many of these noises can you eliminate at any given time?

- Do the same exercise in the quietest room in your house. Record all the sounds again. We are so accustomed to hearing these sounds that we take them for granted.
- Repeat the exercise yet a third time, but this time turn off every noise-producing item in your house. Now what do you hear? Have your child describe the sounds in all three situations. Talk about how you feel in those three situations.

water

Man is a complex being:
He makes deserts bloom and lakes die.

Gil Stein

FRESH WATER

WATER is the basis for all plant and animal life on Earth.

Three-fourths of the Earth's surface is water. Our bodies are 65 percent water. We could live for weeks without food, but only a few days without the water that keeps the blood flowing through our bodies, our joints lubricated, our tissues soft, and our bodies cool. It is essential to our existence.

Water keeps plants upright and transports vital minerals from the soil through the roots to the leaves. The chemical in the leaves, chlorophyll, causes the water to combine with carbon dioxide to produce the plant's food. Water helps to move the food from the leaves to other parts of the plant.

Many desert species of plants and animals have developed adaptive systems which help them to survive when water is scarce. Eventually, however, that system needs to be replenished—with water.

All the Earth's species need this life-giving liquid to stay healthy. We drink it, bathe in it, wash our food (as do some animals) and clothes in it, grow food with it, and cook with it. When we turn on our faucets, we expect an endless supply of fresh, clean water, just as an animal does when approaching a stream for a drink. Without it, we would all cease to exist.

Ninety-seven percent of the Earth's water is in our oceans—and is unusable because of its high salt content. Two percent is frozen in glaciers and ice caps—also unusable because of the difficulty in conveying it. The water we *can* use, the remaining 1 percent, comes from rivers, streams, and lakes, which provide us with about 10 percent of our usable water, and groundwater, which provides the remaining 90 percent.

Groundwater is found beneath the Earth's surface in cracks and spaces between rocks. But due to a lack of understanding of the effects that certain human activities have on groundwater, its purity has become severely jeopardized.

issue

The threat of global warming, a depleted ozone layer, acid rain, and the devastating effects of pollution all seriously affect the future of our water supply. Another critical factor to be considered along with these man-made problems is the fact that the world's drinking water is unevenly distributed around the globe. Much of Africa, the Middle East, parts of Central America, and the western United States are already experiencing the kinds of water shortages that can lead to famine in less developed countries. This problem generally occurs because of inefficient or overly heavy use of water that was in limited supply to begin with.

Historically, water has been treated as an unlimited resource. Water is constantly used and the Earth constantly produces more, as if by magic. This attitude continues to thrive in many cultures, including our own. We need to understand that the Earth's production of fresh water is limited. If educated voices do not speak up, many of these already imperiled areas will face water shortages of dangerous proportions in the not-too-distant future. Sadly, this is already the case in some parts of the world—Ethiopia, for example.

The consumption demands of growing populations will only exacerbate the problems. We must protect what we have to meet those demands. Two dangerous obstacles stand in our way.

Water Pollution

We are mercilessly polluting our fresh water—the very water we drink. Five primary sources of pollution are directly responsible for the situation.

▶ **1** *Industrial Sources.* In the United States, the organic chemical, plastics, and steel industries are responsible for the most serious toxic chemical pollution, whether by direct dumping or as the result of accidents during transportation or manufacturing.

Among the most damaging of the industrial sources are oil spills. These are not only restricted to marine transport. Because factories are often located on riverbanks, any potential industrial accident will seriously damage the nearby river. More than twenty of these spills occur every year.

▶ **2** *Hazardous Waste Disposal.* Very little industrial waste is currently being recycled. Most of it makes its way into injection wells, pits, and landfills. These eventually leach into our groundwater. There are thousands of these waste sites all around the United States, and a large number of them pose a threat to our groundwater systems.

▶ **3** *Agricultural Sources.* Agricultural waste is a major source of pollution all over the world. Chemicals used in crop maintenance, and animal waste, are the leading causes of that pollution. Contaminated runoff from farms greatly affects the groundwater supply.

▶ **4** *Acid Rain.* Precipitation with high levels of sulfuric and nitric acids "kill" water supplies by destroying the plant and animal life that inhabits them, posing a threat to people and animals who use these water sources.

▶ **5** *Acid Mine Waste.* The mining industry, especially the coal industry, is responsible for much stream damage. The drainage from mines is especially acidic and extremely harmful to the life forms inhabiting freshwater streams.

If our water, the very substance which keeps us alive, becomes sick, it follows that all who use it will be adversely affected as well.

A number of studies have been and are being conducted to determine the kinds of risks we face and the illnesses likely to result from contaminated water. Not all the results are in, but the fact that studies need to be made at all should make us question the safety of our water systems. There is a further concern.

Water Waste

As damaging as the contamination aspect is the amount of water we as a society waste. The U.S. population alone consumes 450 billion gallons of water every day! This translates into 150 gallons per day for every man, woman, and child. With our ever-declining safe water sources, it is imperative that we learn how to conserve what we have if we are to expect a continual safe supply of water in the future. Most of what you can do is relatively easy. It just requires some changes in habit and a little forethought.

make a difference!

AROUND THE HOUSE:

▶ **1** The Safe Water Drinking Act protects your right to have the drinking water in your home tested and to know the results of any similar tests being conducted by local governments. For information on having your water tested, contact your local public works office.

▶ **2** Call your water company for the latest information they have about water conservation. Most utility companies are more than happy to help you learn, and usually provide free literature with water-saving tips. This is a good project for an older child. Have him look up the telephone number in the telephone book, or on an old water bill, and call for any available information.

▶ **3** Install faucet aerators. These little gadgets reduce tap flow by 60 percent by infusing the water with air. Using them around the house can help save approximately 6,000 gallons of water per year. It is an inexpensive item, available at most hardware stores. As always, take an interested child along with you to shop for the product and let him help with the installation.

▶ **4** Install a low-flow shower head. It reduces flow by about 75 percent. An average shower consumes about 12 gallons of water per minute. The low-flow shower head reduces this to 3 gallons without affecting the temperature or your comfort.

▶ **5** Install toilet dams. This device helps to cut flush flow by 50 percent and saves approximately 13,000 gallons per year. You may have heard the suggestion to use bricks inside the tank. Beware of this trick. Little pieces of the brick sometimes break off and can clog your system, inviting costly repairs.

- A commercial device is available from Seventh Generation (see Chapter 5).

- A less expensive alternative is to fill a plastic bottle—an empty shampoo or plastic ketchup bottle will do—with rocks. Screw the lid back on and place the bottle inside the toilet tank. Make sure that it is well out of the way of the flushing mechanism. This is a great project for the kids! Be sure to give them a hand in lifting and replacing the toilet tank lid.

- You can always opt for the easiest solution of all, and that is not to flush each time the toilet is used. It requires a little training as to when it is okay not to flush, but once children learn, a great deal of water can be saved. Each flush uses an average of 6 gallons of water.

▶ **6** If you are in the process of building your home, or remodeling a bathroom, consider installing a low-flow toilet. These toilets use between 1 and 1½ gallons per flush, as opposed to the average 5 to 7 gallons a standard toilet uses. Composting toilets are also available (see Chapter 5).

▶ **7** When purchasing a washing machine, consider a front-loading model. They use one-third less water, and two-thirds less soap. Montgomery Ward and White-Westinghouse manufacture reliable models.

▶ **8** Avoid grinding your food in the garbage disposal. Decimated particles enter into the water system and though they are "organic," they do contain bacteria and unsafe particles. It's best to compost such waste, or put it in the trash, though this is the less environmentally sound alternative.

▶ **9** Only run the dishwasher and washing machine when they are fully loaded. The temptation to run the machine (especially the washing machine) with a small load is great, but try to avoid it. It's a tremendous waste of energy and water.

▶ **10** Use only phosphate-free detergents. Liquid detergents generally do not contain any phosphates, while powders do. Be sure to read the labels carefully. Ingredient listing will tell you if there are phosphates in the product.

▶ **11** Save your bath/shower water. One good use for it is to replace the water in the toilet tank when you flush. Just remove the tank lid, flush, and begin filling the tank once the shut-off mechanism has engaged. Keep filling until the "bulb" has risen and shut the intake valve off. You'll know that's happened when the sound of running water stops. This water is also good for washing your car or the family bicycles.

▶ **12** Water household plants with leftover tea or water from steamed or boiled vegetables. Vegetable water contains many nutrients and your house plants will appreciate the added minerals.

▶ **13** Dispose of household chemicals—paint, furniture stripper, paint removers, drain cleaners, etc.—carefully. Contact your local sanitation department for approved landfills, community collection programs, or recycling centers for such toxins. (Read more about this in Chapter 3.)

To eliminate the need to dispose of toxic household chemicals found in cleansers, consider using these alternative, safe organic cleansers. Instead of:

- abrasive powders, use half a lemon dipped in borax to scrub away stains;
- air fresheners, use an open bowl of vinegar;
- ammonia-based cleaners, use a mixture of white vinegar, water, and salt;
- bleach-based cleaners, use borax;
- carpet cleaners, use a light dusting of cornstarch, let settle for one hour, and vacuum as usual;
- disinfectant cleansers, use borax and hot water, or even a mild soap which is effective at killing germs;
- drain cleaners, use a little elbow grease and a plunger, a healthy dose of boiling water, or a mixture of baking soda and vinegar;
- furniture polish, use one part lemon juice and two parts olive or other kind of vegetable oil;
- oven cleaners, use baking soda, fine steel wool, and water;
- silver polish, use baking soda, salt, boiling water, and pieces of aluminum foil (not to rub the silver, but to dissolve in the

water). The combined ingredients help to remove the tarnish. For other metals (copper, brass, pewter, etc.) use vinegar and salt;

• toilet bowl cleaners, use baking soda and a mild soap.

The added benefit of using these natural substances to clean your home is the help your children will be able to give you! You won't have to worry about them inhaling toxic fumes, or splashing toxins on sensitive skin.

▶ **14** Use boiling water and baking soda in your drains not only when they are clogged, but weekly, to help prevent the need for highly toxic "decloggers" and high plumber bills. It will also keep odors from building up.

▶ **15** Double up in the tub. Siblings have fun playing in the tub. If you must bathe them alone, at least save the bath water for the next child.

▶ **16** Don't let the water run when brushing your teeth (2 gallons), shaving (5–10 gallons), or washing the dishes (20 gallons). Wet your toothbrush or the dish and only turn the faucet back on for rinsing purposes.

▶ **17** Take shorter showers. Remember, with an average shower head you will use about 12 gallons per minute. Avoid baths altogether. An average soak in the tub requires about 40 gallons of water.

▶ **18** Don't let the water run for a cold drink. Keep a water bottle in the refrigerator. Make it a house rule that whoever finishes the bottle has to refill it. Collect in a bottle (perhaps an empty milk or juice container) the water that runs every time you are waiting for it to heat up enough to do the dishes. This water can be put in the refrigerator and used for drinking, rinsing the dishes, watering the plants, or filling your pet's water dish.

▶ **19** Have children be on the lookout for leaky faucets and toilets. Make sure they are repaired immediately. Even a tiny leak can waste over 3,000 gallons per year.

OUTSIDE THE HOUSE:

▶ **1** If you must water your lawn, do so after sunset. This will keep the sun from evaporating the water before the soil has had a chance to soak it in.

▶ **2** Avoid watering your lawn in a drought situation. Grass that is turning brown is almost dormant and will not reap any benefits from watering.

▶ **3** Avoid watering your lawn on windy days. The wind can blow the water away.

▶ **4** Pay attention to the weather report. If it looks as if rain is on the way, refrain from watering the lawn and garden. The natural alternative is much more nutritious for your vegetation than chlorine-laden tap water.

▶ **5** Keep a rain barrel somewhere in your yard. Consider removing a length of rain gutter at the side of your house and placing a large receptacle directly underneath to collect the rainwater. This "free" water is a great way to "reuse" water.

▶ **6** Set the blade of your lawn mower at a higher level in the summer. Taller grass retains more moisture than shorter grass.

▶ **7** In the garden, use a watering can for small areas. Using a sprinkler tends to waste water as they are designed to cover larger areas.

▶ **8** Landscape your yard with native plants. They often require less water and resist insect and fungus better than non-native species. Your local nursery will be able to offer some suggestions, or you can pick up a book at the library for more information.

▶ **9** Consider installing a drip irrigation system. The constant watering by "drip" action can help cut garden watering by 50 percent. This method allows soil to remain consistently moist and encourages the production of humus that in turn keeps the soil loose and absorbent.

▶ **10** Avoid lawn fertilizers. They may make your lawn greener, but they leach into and contaminate the groundwater. Consider organic methods. *The Chemical Free Lawn* by Warren Schulz (Rodale Press, 1989) can help you get your lawn "off drugs."

▶ **11** Use mulch around trees and shrubs. Mulch helps to hold in the moisture so you won't have to water as often.

▶ **12** For the truly committed, install a "graywater" tank. (Graywater is water that has been used before.) At a cost of between $200 and $400 for parts (more if you need a sump pump), you can install a system that will collect and redistribute your graywater— water from the dishwasher, washing machine, sinks, etc. This recycled water should be confined to outdoor purposes, however, because of the detergents and bacteria from food that will filter through the system.

Remember that humans are not the only species that require fresh water for survival. Our plant and animal friends are just as dependent on fresh water for survival as we are. What we do to our water affects the lives and environments of every living creature around us.

Wetlands

Wetlands are among the Earth's most important ecosystems, providing critical habitats for many other species. They are characterized by plants inhabiting lowland areas—most of them inland, freshwater swamps and marshes—that become flooded from time to time. A smaller number are coastal saltwater areas. Found on every continent except Antarctica, wetlands exist in every type of climate—from the frozen tundra of the north to the steamy lowlands of the tropics.

Wetlands perform a number of valuable functions in the natural order of life:

- They provide a nesting and breeding area for millions of migratory birds.
- They provide shelter for an abundance of animal and plant life. In fact, they sustain one-third of the nation's endangered and threatened species.
- They support the country's commercial and recreational fisheries as spawning and nursery areas, and often act as sources of nutrients for commercial fisheries in coastal areas.
- They cleanse polluted waters by providing fresh, clean water. Wetlands plants can absorb excess nutrients, neutralize toxins, and prevent them from moving up into the food chain.
- They prevent or regulate flooding by generally acting as a receptacle for floodwaters, which they convey from upstream to downstream points.
- They protect shorelines. Coastal wetlands and inland wetlands adjoining large lakes and rivers reduce the impact of

high tides and waves before they reach the upland areas.
• Millions of years ago, wetlands produced and preserved many of the fossil fuels we now depend on.
• They recharge groundwater aquifers. Aquifers can become seriously and often irreversibly damaged if not replenished before they dry out. Drying out can cause the ground to settle and never be revitalized. This is particularly damaging in agricultural areas that greatly depend on water.

issue

Within the last two hundred years, as much as 50 percent of the wetlands in this country have been filled in to support human activity. Agriculture, oil and gas extraction, forestry, mining, and urbanization are among these wetlands-destroying activities. We've seen this happen especially along the coast of Florida, where acres and acres of wetlands have been filled in to support the development of vacation homes and resorts.

The growth of these activities is causing our wetlands to disappear at an alarming rate. With them will go a vital natural support system. Many species of waterfowl and plants will be lost.

make a difference!

▶ 1 Perhaps the best thing you can do as a family to promote the protection of important wetlands areas is to offer your support— both time and money—to organizations whose function it is to protect them. Listed below are a few organizations which do just that.

Ducks Unlimited, Inc.
One Waterfowl Way
Long Grove, IL 60047
708-438-4300

Wetlands for Wildlife, Inc.
P.O. Box 344
West Bend, WI 53095

The Whooping Crane Conservation Association, Inc.
3000 Meadowlark Dr.
Sierra Vista, AZ 85635
602-458-0971

The Wildfowl Trust of North America, Inc.
P.O. Box 519
Grasonville, MD 21638
301-827-6694

▶ **2** Visit wetlands in your area or while on vacation. Experience for yourself the diversity of life that exists in these beautiful, peaceful areas.

OCEANS

We've talked about the problems facing our freshwater systems and the humans and animals who use them. But what about the oceans and seas that are also home to many of our plant and animal friends? Unfortunately, all is not well with them either.

Consider the oceans that cover nearly 75 percent of the Earth's surface. Beneath the surface of their waters are myriad species of plants and animals. In fact, underwater habitats are just as varied as those on the land. There are huge expanses of underwater deserts and mountain ranges and sea kelp forests, each of which contains a variety of plant and animal species found nowhere else on the planet. The richest and most diverse of these is the tropical coral reef.

The Coral Reef

Coral reefs are delicate, complex ecosystems that require plentiful bright light, a constant flow of clean water, a high saline content, and a minimum water temperature of over 70 degrees Fahrenheit.

Because this environment is so delicate, it is extremely sensitive to environmental changes. The constant flow of clean water that it requires provides nourishment for the life within it. Any disturbance to the flow is detrimental to the reef and to the life it supports.

The importance of this ecosystem rivals that of the rain forest. In fact, it contains more plant and animal groups than any other ecosystem, *including* the rain forest. Here, just as with rain forests, encroaching human development threatens its existence.

Other Marine Ecosystems

It is important to remember that coral reefs along with the other marine ecosystems—salt marshes, mangroves, and estuaries—are the most productive parts of the ocean. They account for well over half of the marine species and almost all of the global fish yield.

Salt marshes are tidal wetlands that are found in temperate areas. Mangroves are their equivalent in tropical areas. Both are habitats for the offshore sea grasses that provide nourishment for ducks and geese in the marshes and for sea turtles and aquatic mammals in the mangroves. The sea grasses also filter out pollution and prevent coastal erosion.

Mangroves are probably the most productive of all coastal ecosystems and are found on over half of the planet's tropical shores. Vast quantities of fish and shellfish live in mangroves, providing food for humans as well as for other marine life.

Estuaries are another critical marine ecosystem. Areas where freshwater rivers meet the salty oceans, they contain the nutrients from both ocean and land that provide sustenance to a vast number of plant and animal species. Their structure allows them to catch and retain pollutants rather than conveying them to the sea. But the increase of these contaminants may be more than the ecosystem can handle, and the resultant threat to marine life is a growing concern.

issue

There are a number of activities that severely threaten the coral reefs and other marine ecosystems. Marine ecosystems are delicately balanced and human activity has had some devastating effects on them.

▶ **1** *Industrial Waste.* Some manufacturers actually have pipelines which carry toxic wastes directly out into rivers and bays.

▶ **2** *Municipal Sewage.* Public sewage treatment plants discharge millions and millions of gallons of sewage into marine waters. In fact, about 35 percent of all U.S. sewage finds its way into these waters.

▶ **3** *Urban Runoff.* Food and solid wastes, lawn chemicals, and construction-site toxins begin their journey in storm sewers, flow on to various waterways, and eventually reach the ocean.

▶ **4** *Algae.* The nitrogen and phosphates that reach marine waters are the result of detergents, fertilizers, and human waste being dumped into the ocean. Algae thrive on these and, depending on their levels, can grow out of control. Large quantities of algae can deplete the oxygen supply, suffocate other species, block the sunlight which affects the growth of still other species, and can also be a toxic substance infiltrating the food chain.

▶ **5** *Acid Rain.* (See discussion under Fresh Water.)

▶ **6** *Development.* Dredging and filling coastal areas for the purpose of building residential communities and resorts completely destroys these marine ecosystems.

▶ **7** *Oil Spills.* Between 3 and 6 million metric tons of oil make their way into oceans yearly. About 1.5 million metric tons are the result of shipping accidents like the *Exxon Valdez* spill in Alaska in 1989. But the largest percentage by far comes from oil tankers washing out their storage tanks with ocean water and releasing the oily water back into the ocean. Oil can damage or kill marine life at every level, from the simplest of plants to wildlife.

▶ **8** *Shipboard Discharges.* Most of these are in the form of plastics and are extremely harmful to marine birds and animals. Some animals mistake plastics for food, others become trapped and entangled in refuse such as plastic fishing nets and six-pack rings (the kind used to hold sodas and beer together).

▶ **9** *Overfishing.* Some of the world's major ocean fisheries are reporting a serious leveling off, others a decline, and still others a total collapse of their yields due to overfishing.

make a difference!

▶ **1** If you own a boat, observe the speed limit so as not to cause excessive disturbance within 500 feet of the shore. Remember that most of the marine life lives relatively close to shore.

▶ **2** Do not dispose of trash overboard. Return it to land and discard it properly.

▶ **3** Exercise your political voice. Let your legislators know that you are not pleased with the state of the world's domestic and wild water. Encourage them to pass protective legislation and impose harsh and well-enforced penalties against polluters.

▶ **4** Exercise your consumer voice. Refuse to support companies that do not engage in safe maritime practices when transporting their goods, especially the oil companies, or that practice unsafe techniques when fishing.

▶ **5** Boycott the purchase of shells and corals (especially black coral). These are vital to the ecosystems they inhabit and excessive collection disrupts the natural balance of that ecosystem.

▶ **6** Visit aquariums and learn about marine life. Knowing what the oceans hold will help you realize the need to protect them. Consider purchasing a family membership which entitles you to participate in the many educational opportunities available—lecture series, outings, films, etc.

▶ **7** If you live in a coastal area, organize a beach cleanup. You'll be surprised how much trash you can collect even on a seemingly well-tended stretch of shoreline. You can do this with a class, the whole school, or even as a family. Do it for the shorebirds and for yourself.

▶ **8** Purchase audio tapes with marine-life themes. Nature Recordings, a company in Washington State, produces a number of fine, high-quality tapes to bring the sea closer to you when you can't be there yourself. They offer such titles as: "The Sea," ninety minutes of ocean waves, tidal pool activity, shorebirds, and fog horns; and "Voices of the Sea," which features a fog whistle, and the songs of whales and dolphins. To obtain further information, contact:

Nature Recordings
P.O. Box 2749
Friday Harbor, WA 98250
206-378-3979

learning activities

▶ **1** To see just how dependent we are on water, try this little experiment. When you get up in the morning, have each family member put a small notepad and a pencil in their pocket (a single piece of paper will do as well). Each time you use water for any reason during the day, make a note of it (i.e., tooth brushing, cleaning the fishbowl, filling ice trays, flushing the toilet). It won't be easy to tell how much water you use, but you'll be surprised at how many times you do use it. Your list should be very long. Think about how much is used multiplied by the members of your household! This is an excellent project for older children.

▶ **2** To learn about the water cycle try this simple experiment. You'll need:

a clear plastic bowl
an empty plastic yogurt cup
a piece of plastic wrap large enough to cover the top of the bowl
and a stone or other "weight"

Place the yogurt container open end up in the middle of the bowl.

Fill the bowl half-full of water (less if the water begins to fill the yogurt cup, which should remain empty).

Cover the bowl with the plastic, making sure it is securely fastened. Try putting a rubber band around the lip of the bowl to keep it in place.

Set the stone or weight in the middle of the plastic cover directly above the yogurt container. The weight of the stone causes the water to collect in one spot over the cup so that it will fall into it.

Place the bowl in a sunny place and watch. You'll soon see how the evaporated water condenses on the underside of the plastic cover and, when enough has collected, falls into the yogurt cup, like rain!

▶ **3** This activity will help your child understand the effects that phosphates have on water. A phosphate is a chemical used to increase the amount of suds that a particular soap will produce, and to make them last longer. You'll need:

a tablespoon
four different brands of laundry or dish detergent
four identical jars with lids
masking tape
scissors
a ruler
a pen
water
a clock or watch

Cut a piece of masking tape the height of the jar and mark one-inch increments.

Put one tablespoon of each detergent into each jar.

Write the name of the detergent on the tape and affix it to the side of the jar.

Fill each jar half-full with water.

Mark the water line on the tape.

Screw on the jar lids and shake vigorously for one minute.

Mark the suds line on the tape. Do this for each of the jars.

Leave the jars alone for ten minutes and then mark the suds line again. Have they gone down? Stayed the same? Which detergents make the least amount of suds? Is this better for the water than the sudsier detergents?

▶ **4** This experiment will help you to test how clean your water is. You'll need:

四 four small, clean jars
four coffee filters
a large jar with a wide mouth
masking tape
a small notebook and a pen

Collect four different kinds of water in the jars. You can use tap water, bottled water, ocean water (if you live near one), rain water, pond water, river water, or water that has collected in a puddle on the street.

Put a piece of masking tape on each jar identifying where it came from.

On four separate sheets in your notebook jot down the characteristics of each water sample, and include information about when you collected it, what the weather was like when you did, etc.

Place a coffee filter in the mouth of the large jar and pour one sample through it. What do you see? Does the filter become discolored by the water? Is there any residue on the filter? Repeat this step using a clean filter for each sample.

Which sample left the most deposit in the filter and which the least? How would you explain your findings?

▶ **5** Make a rainbow! A rainbow is that magical arch of colors that appears when the sun shines after rain. There are seven colors in the rainbow—red, orange, yellow, green blue, indigo, and violet—though often we can only distinguish three or four of them because they blend into one another.

- Pick a warm, sunny day. Put your bathing suit on.
- Direct the hose high into the air so that it forms an arch. As the sun's rays strike each droplet of water, watch for the beautiful colors. This activity would actually be useful if you did it on a lawn or near a garden that needed watering.
- How many colors can you see? Are they always in the same order or do they change? Talk about your rainbow and describe it in your own words. Do you see a pot of gold at the end of this rainbow?

▶ 6 Put on your raincoat and hat and your rubber boots and take a walk in the rain.

- Stick your tongue out. What does it feel and taste like?
- Do the colors of nature look different in the rain? How?
- What kinds of sounds do you hear in the rain?
- Are there any special animals or insects that come out in the rain?
- Does rain have a smell? Does the Earth smell different after it rains?
- Write a story or poem about walking in the rain.
- Tape-record the sound of rain on the roof, on the car, on aluminum drainage pipes, on a swimming pool, etc.

▶ 7 Go whale and dolphin watching, and coastal bird watching! See for yourself how beautiful these creatures are and how they could not survive without their ocean waters.

land

We abuse land because we view it as a commodity, belonging to us. When we see land as a community to which we belong, we may begin to use it with love and respect.

Aldo Leopold

IT is shamefully clear that there are serious problems with our relationship to the land. Philosophers throughout time have challenged us to confront our denial of abusive behavior toward the land and our resistance to changing that behavior, yet their words customarily fell—and continue to fall—on deaf ears. Ancient religions and the Native American tribes all understood (the Native Americans still understand) the interconnectedness of all living things and the fundamental necessity of land. Western modern thought has never quite absorbed that ancient and basic precept.

In 1949, ecologist Aldo Leopold wrote his classic treatise on land issues, "The Land Ethic," in *A Sand County Almanac*. He saw, as few others did at the time, that the life-supporting systems of the land—the interdependent relationships of air, land, water, plants, and animals—were breaking down and showing signs of wear. Today, nearly fifty years later, it is no longer necessary to be a visionary to see the signs of the breakdown that Leopold foretold. As evidence of the effects of global abuse mounts, our common sense is increasingly offended by the disparity between the situation as it *should be* and what, in reality, it actually *is*. The chilling suspicion grows that we have allowed our environmentally abusive habits to go too far.

That we have allowed it to come this far indicates that our way of thinking about the land, and our actual relationship to it, are both deeply flawed. If the health of the land on which all living things depend is to be preserved, we will have to learn to think of it not as mere property but as "community," and of ourselves not as owners but members of this vast community. For we are all interconnected, rich and poor, white and black, young and old, friend and foe, animal and plant, water and air, soil and sun.

Our sustainability as a species on this planet depends upon how we confront our denial of these global issues, and how this denial affects our decision-making powers. Leopold suggests that the root cause of our predicament is even deeper, entwined with our basic assumptions, attitudes, and beliefs—the fundamental values that make up the dominant world view. What we are a part of today is an evolution of these values. We are beginning, ever so gently, to realign our old world view with the reality of what is happening to the natural world. The tips and projects that follow this section are designed to help nurture these changing values in our children, for their period of evolution will not be so gentle. The global time clock is ticking at an ever-accelerating pace, challenging us daily to change our ways.

POPULATION GROWTH

The size of the human population affects virtually every environmental condition on the Earth. Today, over 5 billion people inhabit the planet, compared to 1 billion in the nineteenth century. The rate of increase is so dramatic that unless the use of birth control methods increases, the world population will exceed an estimated 6 billion before the year 2000; 10 billion by 2025; and 14 billion by the end of the next century. If this rate is allowed to continue, the number of people on the planet will *double in less than forty years* and seriously tax or entirely deplete our planet's natural resources. All this will happen during our lifetimes, creating problems even more severe for our children's generation.

The continual increase in demand for resources leads inevitably to increased pollution and waste problems. More energy is used, escalating the problems of global warming, acid rain, oil spills, and nuclear waste. More land is required for agriculture, homes, and factories, contributing to deforestation and soil erosion. Political conflicts arising over ownership of resources will lead to more civil wars between countries. And species will continue to become extinct at an astronomical rate due to loss of habitat. Population growth appears to contribute significantly to the tragedy of environmental degradation.

Some experts describe the bottom line in terms of sustainability. It has been suggested that a society cannot truly be sustainable if it consumes renewable resources faster than they can be replenished. In other words, an overpopulated society clears forests and uses water supplies faster than they have time to renew themselves. Measured in this way, the world is already overpopulated, and we all have a responsibility to support efforts to find viable solutions that impose as little change as possible on cultural and social mores.

As Aldo Leopold stresses in his writings, every condition is interconnected. We cannot solve this one problem of overpopulation by suggesting unnatural solutions such as mandatory sterilization after having one child, and then expect everything else to work itself out. Perhaps if we can expand our public policy agenda to question our value system, we will make the cultural changes necessary to ensure that there will be fertile land and wilderness left for our children's children. The challenge is our choice, and the next generation's inheritance.

It is not our intention to pass judgment, but rather to engage people in an active dialogue of what is most valuable in life. When we look at population growth and its consequences we must take responsibility for our own actions and instill these values as we raise the children of the future.

make a difference!

▶ Choose a socially responsible approach to population growth.

learning activity

▶ How does the population grow? You will need some crayons and paper for this simple illustration of population growth.

- Have your child draw a picture of himself in the middle of the top portion of a piece of paper. Underneath he should draw two lines in either direction (yes, you are creating a family-tree diagram) and pictures of two children attached to those lines.
- Beneath each child, draw two more lines and drawings of four grandchildren. Finally, draw two more lines below each of the four grandchildren, to form a picture of the eight great-grandchildren.
- Turn the paper over and attempt to build the same family tree, only beneath each person draw four lines and four more people. Discuss how many great-grandchildren they might have if each family member had four children. Talk about what would happen to the planet if all the people in the world created large families generation after generation.

What are the various land issues affected by this increasing, demanding population?

SOIL

Throughout time people have tried to find riches within the Earth—gold and other minerals, gems, and fossil fuels. Ironically, these riches will someday run out while the real wealth, the soil itself, remains.

Today that soil is at risk. Strip-mining, deforestation, poor farming practices, hazardous waste, acid rain, and overpopulation all challenge our desire to preserve our food-producing soil.

Most soil consists mainly of small rock particles broken down through the ages by the action of wind, water, and ice. Fertile soil also contains water, air, plant roots, decayed plants and animals, as well as living organisms such as bacteria and earthworms. Historically, the soil has been our direct means of growing vegetables, fruits, grains to make bread, grass to graze our livestock, and trees to provide our lumber. It has been estimated that our soil supplies two-thirds of all the raw materials used by industry.

As paper and housing demands increase, mountain after mountain is destroyed by clear-cut lumbering. The trees that once held the topsoil in place are gone, no longer able to prevent the soil from washing away. The barren wilderness becomes scarred forever since it is unlikely that the eroded soil will ever sustain such a grand forest of trees again. Soil erosion pollutes our lakes and streams, threatening fish and contaminating our drinking water. Once people actually witness the devastation of clear-cutting, a commitment to paper recycling becomes a daily necessity. Take as an example the Sunday issue of our newspapers. It is no longer acceptable that more than half a million trees are cut down to produce just one Sunday's worth of newspapers read in this country when we have the technology to use recycled paper for printing our newspapers.

Additional stress is placed on the soil by the increasing demands placed upon it and our poor conservation practices. Topsoil can erode, blow, and wash away, stripping the land of its life-giving qualities. Such conditions have resulted in the desertification of vast areas of our planet, though we have the technology to prevent further destruction if we act wisely. In the United States alone, erosion from wind and water removes about three billion tons of soil from American croplands each year, reducing land productivity and carrying polluting pesticide residues into our water sources.

Sustainable farming practices of the future must include an ability to grow sufficient crops while rebuilding, or at least not depleting, the natural resources of soil and water on which the crop depends. At present this is difficult to do because 85 percent of all topsoil in the United States is directly associated with the raising of livestock. This land use is divided between fields for grazing and land specifically used for the cultivation of animal feed crops. Because of the vast resources required for livestock breeding, experts suggest a vegetarian diet as the single most important step a person can take to save the environment. (This issue will be discussed further in Chapter 6.) These valuable resources would be better served if we enhanced our farming capabilities and made it easier for less developed countries to feed themselves. This is an ethical land issue and one that is not likely to take hold until millions more people starve and our soil and water resources have become stressed to their limit.

A change in values is not yet apparent in our present society. Government actions thus far have not supported any sustainable farming practices. In fact, one major culprit of soil abuse is sanctioned by the U.S. government. National farm policy rewards farmers for "monoculture"—growing a single crop such as corn on hundreds of acres, year after year, even though such methods are chemically intensive and environmentally unsound. Monoculture strips the soil of particular nutrients and requires the excessive use of chemicals to keep the soil balanced.

Chemically intensive agriculture depends upon air-polluting fertilizers and toxic pesticides to produce a healthy crop year after year. These practices continue despite scientific evidence that shows, in most cases, chemical-free agriculture to be as productive as those methods requiring the use of pesticides.

Alternative agricultural practices will have to be developed if our true "gold," our soil, is to survive. As consumers, we can all help encourage a transition to environmentally sensitive agriculture by thoughtful shopping and eating habits.

make a difference!

▶ Test your soil annually. Call your county extension service for information on how to do this. Determine what is missing and attempt to replenish it by composting those nutrient-rich food scraps and adding them to your soil. Instead of dousing your soil with chemicals, practice organic gardening methods only.

learning activities

▶ 1 *Make Soil.* This is an activity that will show children the value of land, its delicate balance, and the consequences of imbalance. You'll need three flower pots or buckets, a shovel, and a spot in your garden where you can dig a hole. This project is best tackled after it rains and the soil is still moist.

- Dig a hole! Be careful to save the rich layer of topsoil. Topsoil is a dark brown humus, organic matter which has been well aerated by worms and insects.
- Fill the first pot with a sample of the rocky material from the bottom layer of your hole. This is called parent material.
- Fill the second pot with earth from inside your hole. This is the subsoil layer. It is lighter in color and has a high mineral content combined with organic matter from decomposed plants and insects, called humus.
- Fill the third pot with the three different layers of soil. Line

the bottom with the parent material followed by subsoil and finally with a layer of the rich topsoil.

• Plant some flower seeds in each of the pots. Place them in the same spot in the sun, water when necessary, and observe how they grow throughout the week. How are the flowers growing differently in each of the pots? Which one is doing the best? Which is doing the worst? Explain the concept of soil erosion and how plants and trees will not be able to grow as well when there is no topsoil.

▶ **2** *Save the Soil.* Soil erosion has carved our scenic canyons and waterways. Through these two simple activities children will become aware of the effects of water on the soil.

• Build two mounds, one of sand and one of dirt. Pour water on each of the mounds and discuss what happens to the soil and sand.

• Build a mound in an unplanted part of the garden, just as you would if there were plants in the soil. Water this part of the garden just as you would the part with plants in it.
What happens to the soil where there are no plants?
What happens where there are plants?
Discuss the fact that plant roots help to keep soil in place. The roots need the soil to help conduct the water up through their stems.

Let the discussion include the larger picture. How can a forest survive if erosion washes away that important layer of topsoil? How can new trees take root? How will soil stay in place if there are no plants and trees?

▶ **3** *Grow a Worm Farm.* This will enable you to understand how worms can help your compost heap and your garden by aerating the soil, a process which helps water and nutrients move around in the earth. You will need:

an old glass jar, fishbowl, or aquarium
a shovel or trowel
moist topsoil and sand
dead leaves or grass clippings
worms (try digging in the garden after a rainfall, or under some rocks)
an old bandanna or a paper bag

Layer the soil and sand in your jar, alternating an inch of each. Sprinkle some water as you layer, leaving two inches at the top for crumpled leaves or grass clippings.

Before you put on the top layer of leaves, drop in the worms (usually you can find them if you dig your soil from a garden).

Cover the worms with the leaves and an old bandanna or a paper bag. Place the jar in a dark area so the worms think they are underground.

Check the experiment after a few days and notice the tunnels that the worms have built. Explain how earthworms help the soil by "aerating"—allowing air to circulate through the soil, which enhances plant growth.

Look for piles of fine soil that has been digested by the worms. These little piles are called "castings" and provide excellent nourishment for your garden plants.

When you have finished observing the worms, make sure they are put back in the ground. They will be much happier and so will your garden.

PESTICIDES

Why are we so afraid of insects damaging our food and industrial crops when our real fear should be the hazardous pesticides we use to kill them? Pesticides, which include insecticides, herbicides, and fungicides, are a group of poisons used for killing or repelling crop-destructive insects. Each year, more than 4 billion pounds of pesticides are used worldwide. Only on rare occasions have any of these pesticides been tested for long-term health effects. We are all subjects in this absurd experiment.

Every year nearly 2 million people worldwide suffer from pesticide poisoning. Pesticide exposure can cause cancer, birth defects, and damage to body organs. Children often receive greater pesticide exposure because of their size, their increased metabolic rate (the speed with which a body burns energy), and their greater consumption of food and air, pound per pound, than adults.

Once distributed, pesticides can harm or perhaps even kill innocent people or animals. An added problem is that they often kill nontargeted creatures that may actually be beneficial to a crop. In areas of heavy pesticide use, poisonings of birds, mammals, and fish are common. Some of the more persistent chemicals may remain dangerous for up to twenty years, leaching into underground water supplies. In the United States alone, pesticides have been found in groundwater supplies in twenty-six states.

Ironically, over the years, many insect species have become resistant to insecticides, necessitating higher doses and the increased application of even more dangerous chemicals. Over the last fifty years, pesticide use has increased dramatically—yet crop *loss* has nearly doubled.

The ultimate irony is that U.S. law currently allows any pesticide to be exported as long as the importing country is notified of its regulatory status. As a result, many of the pesticides that are banned or restricted in the United States because of their known danger to our health and the environment are exported to developing countries. In many cases, the farm workers who apply these chemicals do not even know the risks or protect themselves because they are unable to read the English labels. It is estimated that 70 percent of the pesticides exported to developing countries are used in the production of goods imported back into the United States.

The best solution for pesticide problems is source reduction. Make an effort to explore and at least try alternative natural solutions before purchasing these hazardous products.

make a difference!

▶ **1** Try nonchemical forms of pest control.

▶ **2** If you have a pet and it—and your home—is badly infested with ticks or fleas, try a natural solution before resorting to hazardous pesticides. Place pine needles, fennel, or rosemary in the doghouse or underneath your pet's bedding. Wash your animal periodically with salt water and avoid using flea collars whenever possible.

▶ **3** Use nontoxic pest control remedies first before buying the toxic solutions. Try cedar chips instead of mothballs, cayenne pepper to keep the ants away, a flyswatter for flies, a dish of beer to tackle fruit flies, and make your own "roach motels" by using a glass jar filled with some food and lined with grease to catch the insects inside. The following company makes a "low-impact" line of pest control products for your home and garden:

Safer, Inc.
189 Wells Ave.
Newton, MA 02159

As a society of consumers, we have been raised to take convenience for granted. Technology has often blurred our vision and common sense. Congratulate yourself and your child for every small change that you are willing to make. This Earth-conscious buying is not easy. It is a lifelong learning process.

UNPROTECTED LANDS

The environmental pressure to support an ever-growing meat-eating population puts our greatest treasures at risk—the land areas that remain undeveloped and, unfortunately, unprotected. Unprotected lands receive the polluted water runoff from pesticides and stand available for exploitation despite their wilderness value.

Caves

These fragile underground land areas are a valuable museum of our past. Because of their stable environments, caves can preserve evidence of past human and animal activity. Important clues about past civilizations are found in caves every year. As with any archaeological site, the exact positioning of remains and soil layers (to help determine the age of a particular site) are valuable only so long as the cave remains undisturbed. Vandalism—ranging from the casual visitor who leaves trash in the cave, to the prankster who paints on walls, and the organized professional who removes rock formations for profit—often obliterates the cave's unique and important scientific information. There are other human factors at work as well.

- Water pollution from raw sewage, industrial waste, pesticides, farming, and landfill contamination can pollute the lifeblood of caves—their water. Many rare cave animals are threatened by this pollution, as are those people who rely on caves for drinking water.

- Dam construction has been responsible for the flooding of many of these forgotten, underground treasures. This practice has, in many cases, killed all cave animals, halted the ongoing geological processes, and made caves inaccessible. In most cases, the economic and environmental impact studies for these projects failed to consider the cave resources. Only rarely are caves assessed for "value" before they are destroyed.

- Limestone quarrying also has the potential to utterly destroy caves. Even in those cases where the preservation of caves is considered, removal of nearby or overlying stone can cause the cave to collapse.

- Forestry threatens caves since sawdust and other by-products enter caves via their waterways. These sediments act like cement, clogging smaller streams and strangling the very lifeblood of the cave, its water.

Caves continue to be an exciting source of new scientific knowledge, and we can benefit from the unique species of life that flourish in darkness: Bats, with their bat guano (bat droppings), provide a source of high-quality fertilizer, and the moldlike bacteria found in many caves can be used to produce a wide variety of valuable antibiotics. Caves and their myriad inhabitants deserve our attention and our protection.

Government Lands
There are other forgotten and unprotected lands around the world that warrant a mention. In the United States alone, vast areas of land—over 175 million acres—are overseen by the Bureau of Land Management (BLM) *without* the benefit of a management plan or special designation as a national park or sanctuary. The battle is waged for how to best preserve—or exploit—these lands.

In addition to their incredible wealth of natural beauty, BLM wilderness areas also hold commodities such as natural gas, coal, petroleum, and many minerals. Though much of this land is already being exploited for its riches as a result of government permission, the fight to protect the remaining wilderness rages on. Unlike national parks, forests, and seashores, government-owned BLM lands are unprotected. The questions remain: Can we use this land and still preserve its integrity and natural beauty for the benefit of our future generations? Can we allow it to continue to be used for political favors? Some conservation groups suggest that without vigorous cooperation from government these wilderness areas and their many species of wildlife will be lost forever. The government holds these wildlands in trust for future generations. Sitting idly by and watching them be misused and left to the devices of strip mine operators and logging companies is unacceptable and unwise.

For more information about BLM lands, contact the Wilderness Society (see Chapter 9), and for information about caves, contact the :

National Speleological Society
Cave Ave.
Huntsville, AL 35810
205-852-1300

WASTE

The population growth and resulting strain on our natural resources has forced us to deal with the ever-present and growing problem of waste management.

Handling trash has been an issue requiring our attention for hundreds of years. The usual method has been simply to put it somewhere where it cannot be seen or smelled, or to burn it. Over the years, few refinements have been introduced to this method. We still dump and burn, but in more recent history we have started to convert various forms of trash into something else, or to reuse it. The biggest challenge we face now is actually source reduction, or minimizing the volume we produce to begin with.

Dumping

Historically, dumping has been mankind's first choice for waste disposal. It was not until the threat of disease became obvious that people began to remove their garbage or move away from it. Landfills are now the number one method of solid waste disposal. We can no longer get away from the problem. Many of today's landfills have reached their capacity. They are covered over with dirt and grass, yet their impact upon the environment continues unseen. Picture a garbage dump with thousands of inky pens, leaky batteries, old oil cans, discarded drain cleaners, and silver polishes lurking beneath its surface. As water passes through the garbage and into the soil, it carries with it some of the residue from these hazardous materials. The products of this continuous leaching seep into the ground and poison our water supplies. What will happen to us when we use that water?

The Environmental Protection Agency has identified more than a hundred potentially harmful substances in landfill leachate. Some experts estimate that each day—to cite just one example—more than 1 million gallons of this leachate oozes into underground waterways beneath "Fresh Kills Landfill," the high-rise dump built on the ecologically sensitive salt marshes along the shores of Staten Island in New York. Multiply this volume of leached material by the 5,500 landfills across America, and the thousands more around the world, and you may want to reconsider the tap water you drink.

Gas emissions from landfills are also a growing concern. People not only argue vehemently from an aesthetic perspective when landfills are proposed for their backyards, they also fear living with the horrible smell. Methane, the primary landfill gas, traps twenty-five times more infrared energy than carbon dioxide does, contributing significantly to the global warming crisis. Methane emissions from U.S. landfills alone are estimated to contribute as much as 2 percent to the entire global buildup of greenhouse gases. This estimate easily exceeds the amount of carbon dioxide expelled by 10 million automobiles.

Despite the horror of methane gas emissions, new landfill sites are being built with comprehensive gas-collection systems and leachate tanks. It has been suggested that if landfill methane was collected and processed for energy recovery, it could provide for up to 5 percent of worldwide natural gas consumption, or 1 percent of the energy demand in the United States alone. In fact, solid waste engineers argue that with new technology they can build safe, energy-efficient landfills that will eventually become ecological oases once nature has its way.

community action!

Communities sometimes convert their retired dumps into golf courses, ski resorts, or amusement parks. In Hackensack, New Jersey, for example, workers have begun to restore a landfill to something resembling its natural state. Landscapers are attempting to transform six acres of a closed landfill into grass meadows and young woodlands. This experimental project is intended to test the adaptability of various plant species to the thin layer of nonirrigated, unfertilized soil and the dry, windy conditions typical of a landfill, and to provide food and shelter for songbirds, rabbits, mice, and raccoons.

The area, containing 215,000 cubic yards of garbage, was sealed with a synthetic membrane made from recycled plastic soda bottles that might otherwise have been buried. The bottles were processed into a material that looks similar to the artificial turf of a golf putting green. The mesh formed from the bottles prevents nearly 15,000 cubic yards of topsoil from sliding off the steep slopes of the landfill.

In a few years, groves of green ash and red cedar are expected to grow along the landfill's crown. A meandering footpath is already edged with dogwood and sumac and offers a sweeping view, all too rare in this densely populated area. Eventually, the experimental park may point the rest of the world toward salvaging the thousands of acres of meadowlands and wetlands that were once dismissed as unsightly, unsanitary, and ultimately unusable—except for garbage.

make a difference!

▶ **1** Walk lightly on the land. Leave your path cleaner than you found it. Challenge yourself to take the time to walk with a bag and pick up the mess left by an ignorant neighbor.

▶ **2** Avoid landfill abuse. Use cloth instead of disposable diapers, cloth rags instead of paper towels, cloth napkins instead of paper. Each time you refuse to purchase a disposable product, reward yourself with a pat on the back—or a dish of Ben and Jerry's ice cream (in support of an environmentally conscious business).

Burning

Burning waste has evolved over the years into high-tech inciner-ation. Huge state-of-the-art furnaces called "waste to energy" plants burn our trash and, at the same time, heat water into steam that turns a turbine and makes electricity. This generated elec-tricity is then sold back to electric companies to reduce costs.

Although incinerators reduce the amount of trash that is burned by about 70 percent, the leftover 30 percent is highly toxic ash which still has to be buried. Emissions from incinerators create further air pollution problems such as the ones briefly discussed in Chapter 1.

Incineration releases toxic materials into our land and atmo-sphere. Landfills leach chemicals into our waterways. And both incineration and landfills contribute to air pollution and global warming. This leaves waste reduction as a primary goal in our new waste management regime. Practicing the Three Rs—Reduce, Reuse, and Recycle—should be at the cornerstone of our waste management plans. (See Chapter 5 for more information on the Three Rs.)

make a difference!

▶ Consider what you burn in your fireplace or campfire. Avoid burning toxic materials like plastics, Styrofoam, glossy colored papers, and chemically treated wood.

WASTE REDUCTION

By the year 2025, when 10 billion people are likely to live on this planet, the population will generate an estimated 400 billion tons of solid waste every year—enough to bury Los Angeles, California, under 100 meters of trash—unless waste reduction is practiced.

Junk mail, the unsolicited and unwanted advertising, catalogs, and questionnaires that clog our mailboxes every day, accounts for an estimated 2 million tons of paper waste each year in the United States. The most offensive and frustrating aspect of junk mail is that it is a lucrative, money-making business for many companies. Our privacy is rarely a consideration and mailing lists are bought and sold with frequent and annoying regularity. Some of these businesses set up at trade shows or use sweepstakes applications as a method of obtaining names and addresses. If you order merchandise from a mail-order catalog your name becomes "fair game" to sell elsewhere, unless you authorize the company to withhold your personal information. To reduce junk mail in your home you will have to keep precycling concepts in mind. Avoid giving out your name and address on sweepstakes forms or over the phone in telecommun ications interviews. You can even send back some junk mail at the sender's expense in any prepaid return envelope that is included. In fact, this is a good idea if you wish to be assured that your name will be removed from that particular mailing list. Do not hesitate to send a note along with the returned mail asking the sender to take your name off the mailing list. Reducing this kind of useless abuse of our resources is a crucial step in our waste reduction plan.

Another enormous waste problem is created by the 18 billion disposable diapers thrown away annually in the United States. The problem is exacerbated by the fact that the diseases of past generations will once again become a threat. It is a known fact that infant excrement contains some or all of over one hundred viruses, including polio and hepatitis from vaccine residue, and that these continue to survive in the landfills for years. These viruses are potentially dangerous to sanitation workers and the general population, through groundwater leachate and what may be carried by insects and rodents.

Waste reduction is defined as any strategy which minimizes the need for disposal. It includes reducing the amount of waste generated, diverting materials from the waste stream, and preserving material resources. We can put these strategies to use in our own homes, making them second nature and a common habit for our children as they grow. There are five strategies we can integrate into a personal waste reduction plan:

▶ 1 Reuse.
▶ 2 Remanufacture.
▶ 3 Recycle.
▶ 4 Compost.
▶ 5 Source reduction.

Reuse

Reuse of items in their original form, such as clothing, margarine tubs, refillable bottles, and bags, can be an easy addition to your home waste management plan. Creating an organized storage system, and making an effort to give away rather than dispose of what you cannot use, is a simple guideline for reuse. Most schools, day care centers, and recreation departments welcome the collection of salvageable containers that generally go into the trash. Toilet paper rolls, Styrofoam meat-trays, egg cartons, and bottle caps are all treasured arts and crafts supplies that are sure to be enthusiastically received.

Reuse avoids resource depletion and reduces energy consumption by bypassing the manufacturing process. Simple actions such as carrying your own coffee mug to meetings at work and rinsing out water glasses instead of using paper ones all contribute to a conscientious waste management routine.

Remanufacture

The remanufacture of products is a difficult, not always economical option in our current throw-away society. Remanufacture conserves the initial invested value of the manufacturing process by rebuilding used products—replacing only worn-out parts instead of manufacturing an entirely new product. When the motor in your vacuum cleaner burns out, for example, rather than buying a whole new appliance, just have the motor replaced. Remanufacturing techniques are used extensively in the auto parts industry, which continues to set an example for other product lines.

As consumers we can choose well-made, reliable products built by manufacturers committed to providing extended service for their products. We may end up spending more money for such things as cameras, home appliances, toys, and gifts, but the investment supports a conscientious waste reduction plan that benefits the entire planet. The idea of buying such disposable technology as throw-away cameras, for example, stands in direct defiance of our goals for remanufacture.

make a difference!

▶   Mend and repair instead of discarding and replacing broken appliances, clothes, and toys.

Recycle

If you have not already organized a recycling effort in your home, the actual visual results of waste reduction when you do so will amaze you. After just one week of separating out your glass, metal, plastics, newspaper, cardboard, and white paper you will find your trash receptacle less than half full. If you were a two-green-garbage-bags-a-week family, you may notice that dropping to one bag or even less.

By returning products to their raw material components and using them to supplement or replace virgin materials in the manufacture of a new product is by far the most commonsensible and energy-saving waste reduction technique, and one whose time has come.

Everything is recyclable. The problem up to now has been to find markets for these recycled materials and an economical process to support the industry. As the nonsustainable use of virgin materials begins to threaten our planet, manufacturers are slowly discovering the cost-effective, marketable value of using and reusing recycled materials. Communities are realizing that recycling can be a cost-effective practice because they pay less to dump less.

Perhaps the greatest irony of all lies in the fact that at some point in the future, if we continue at our current rate of consumption, our natural resources will one day run out and we may actually be forced to excavate our landfills to reclaim the valuable treasures found in them.

The bauxite ore used to make aluminum cans is estimated to last only another two to three hundred years. We are already harvesting trees faster than we can grow them. And the oil that so many men and women have lost their lives fighting for in recent times is expected to last only thirty-five years at our present rate of consumption.

make a difference!

▶ 1 Donate old magazines to schools, hospitals, health club reading shelves, or dentists' and doctors' waiting rooms.
▶ 2 Take hangers back to the dry cleaners, plastic and rubber pots back to the nursery, shopping bags back to the store. Returning reusables contributes to waste reduction. If the businesses won't

take them back, ask why and suggest that if they do not recycle you will no longer do business with them.

▶ **3** Set up your home recycling program! (Keep in mind there are many ways to do this. We do not provide you with any glamorous options, just a basic, somewhat unattractive, yet practical setup that you can hone to meet your own needs.)

- Start by making a few phone calls. Check Appendix 2 for the state recycling agency or association in your area. They can bring you up to date on what is recyclable in your area.
- Next, call your community waste management office and request specific local information about recycling. Many areas have curbside recycling that requires special containers and various sorting procedures. As a backup, determine where the nearest recycling center is. Find out if they take the recyclables that are not picked up with your curbside trash. Ideally you will want to recycle everything at one location rather than complicate your life by delivering aluminum to one center and newspapers to another. Cardboard seems to comprise the bulk of family trash and is recyclable in most areas although it is rarely included in curbside pickup.
- Find containers to hold your recyclables. Cardboard boxes work quite well as do plastic laundry baskets or trash cans. Better yet, reuse something—like an empty milk crate. A container with a handle for easy transport will make getting the recyclables to their final destination a little easier. If you buy large buckets of laundry soap or have access to large paint buckets or the pickle buckets used by the food service industry, attempt to reuse them. Buy an attractive container if it will provide extra encouragement for you to initiate a recycling program in your home. The moveable carts offered in many environmental magazines are great for curbside pickup, but are not easy to get into many of today's smaller cars. Baskets look pretty but they get very dirty after months of waste collection.
- Find a convenient site to keep your containers. Keeping them near the kitchen is generally a reasonable choice since most of the waste is generated there. If storage space is a problem, consider a two-step system that utilizes a small

attractive receptacle in the kitchen and larger buckets or boxes out in the garage or in the basement.

• Call in the kids and discuss the new routine. They can participate by rinsing out what remains in the recyclables and making labels to identify the contents of the various collection containers. Keeping the recyclables separated at home will save you time at the recycling center. Have the kids choose and write down what they will do in the home waste reduction plan. Draw up a family contract and have everybody sign.

• Children can also participate in the preliminary dismantling of certain recyclables by squashing cans, flattening boxes, and binding newspapers with string. Not only will this make it easier for you to store them, the transportation will be made much simpler as well. If you are able to recycle white paper and newspaper, keep them separate because it is difficult and often messy when they are mixed in with the bottles, cans, and plastics.

• Save some energy and have some fun. Call a friend and drive to the recycling center together. Plan a trip every few weeks when you are sure to have a full load. Take the kids along. They will grow up considering recycling a part of their daily routine and will be more apt to continue the practice as adults.

▶ 4 Know your recyclables. It's important to know which materials, at this point in time, are suitable and accepted by recyclers.

METALS

Aluminum cans are currently the most valuable recyclables, worth up to $1,000 per ton. Making cans from recycled aluminum cuts air pollution by 95 percent, yet Americans continue to throw away enough aluminum to rebuild our entire commercial air fleet every three months.

Contact the Reynolds Aluminum hotline at 800-228-2525 regarding questions about recyclable aluminum. They take it all: foil, pie tins, storm doors, automobile transmissions, window frames, aluminum cookware, old lawn chairs, and other aluminum scrap. If you are not sure of the metal content of a certain product remember that aluminum will not stick to a magnet.

Tin, steel, and iron are recyclable as well. If they are not easy to unload in your area try looking in the phone book under "Scrap Metal," or contact your state recycling office. If you want to be certain of the steel content of a can, test it with a kitchen magnet (the magnet should stick). Other metal recyclables that often go out with the trash are clothes hangers, water heaters, old cars, plumbing fixtures, broken tools, play equipment, bike frames, garbage cans, ducts and vents, chairs, paint cans, pots, pans, and other appliances. For more information about scrap metal contact the:

Institute of Scrap Recycling Industries, Inc.
1627 K St., N.W.
Washington, D.C. 20006–1704
202-466-4050

GLASS

Glass is made of sand, soda ash, limestone, and feldspar. All these resources are mined, and our land is stripped in the search for them. Ton after ton of resources can be saved by recycling glass.

Before glass is shipped from a recycling center to manufacturers, it is usually separated by color and broken into "cullet," a form of broken glass that takes up less space and is easier to clean and transport. Never put pottery, window glass, drinking glasses, mirrors, Pyrex baking dishes, glass coffee pots, or glass lenses into a glass recycling bin. These kinds of glass can ruin the entire batch because they melt at different temperatures. If you need to recycle odd shades of glass, toss them into the brown or green glass receptacles, where it will generally be accepted. In most cases, recyclers go to great lengths to keep the clear glass "clean." For more information on glass recycling, contact:

The Glass Packaging Institute
1801 K St., N.W., Suite 1105-L
Washington, D.C. 20006
202-887-4850

PAPER

Paper in one form or another comprises the bulk of our trash.

Newsprint: It is estimated that if we recycled even half of our newsprint (the paper used for newspaper) each year in the United States, we would be able to reduce our garbage-hauling fleet by 3,200 trucks. Newsprint is one of the easiest products to recycle. As a general rule, tying newspapers together is unnecessary. Newspaper fits well in a paper bag, cardboard box, or paper shopping bag with handles. If your local recycling program will not recycle the bags, consider using the reusable canvas shopping bags as a convenient tote. Keep the newsprint clean and dry, and avoid the temptation to add junk mail to the pile. Much of it contains glossy papers that are not always recyclable.

White paper: Typical business-stock paper has already been bleached and needs to be separated from newsprint and "brown" paper (i.e., cardboard). "White" paper is worth twice as much as colored ledger paper (i.e., yellow legal pads) and is prized by recyclers because it is usually a strong stock that holds up well to the chemicals used in the recycling process and produces a good-quality paper the second time around. The process of recycling white bleached office paper reduces the amount of rebleaching and cuts down on dioxin (a by-product of bleaching) in our water.

White paper includes computer paper, typing paper, stationery, index cards, copier paper, and white envelopes (peel out any plastic windows; lick-and-stick glue is okay). Some recyclers will accept white paperboard (any product cardboard box that is white on the inside). Usually no adhesives (i.e., labels and "Post-its"), fax paper, carbonless copy paper, or blueprints are accepted. These papers have chemical coatings and must be dealt with separately.

Brown paper: In a broad sense this includes paper grocery bags, corrugated cardboard (i.e., mail-order and pizza delivery boxes), and paperboard with a brown interior (i.e., most cereal and cracker boxes). Sometimes recyclers will also accept odd cardboard like toilet paper tubes, manila envelopes, egg cartons, etc. Check with the recycler for details.

Boxes are bulky and pile up quickly. Flatten them before recycling. No waxed cardboard or foam packing chips are acceptable. Cardboard needs to be clean and stripped of any plastic tapes and foreign material.

Glossy paper: This is the least popular of the recyclable papers because all the coating material must be removed. The "gloss" is achieved by a process that involves the use of clay to achieve the shine. The clay, when separated from the paper during the recycling process, can clog the recycling equipment and cause damage. However, some recyclers do use equipment with an adapted reclaimer and will take your magazines and other glossy papers. Find out before including this paper with the other kinds.

Magazines, mail-order catalogs, and glossy junk mail fall into this "unwanted" category. Precycling efforts, such as reading your favorite magazine and catalog at the library, are suggested if you cannot locate a recycler who will accept the glossy waste paper.

Phone books: An unpopular recycling item because of their size, phone books take up a large amount of landfill space and are starting to be recycled in many areas as a result. Contact the phone company first to see if they are supporting a recycling effort. The problem with recycling phone books centers around the glue and glossy coupon pages that clog machinery at the recycling plants. In some cases, if you separate the pages from the glossy cover, you can send it through with brown or mixed paper.

PLASTICS

There are almost fifty kinds of plastic used in manufacturing and not all are being recycled. The most popular types of plastic are PET, HDPE, PVC, LDPE, PP, and PS.

The trick to recycling plastic is in knowing how to read the recycling code on the bottom of the container. The universal recycling triangle of arrows is your first clue. Inside the symbol is a number. This coding system helps you and the recycler reuse plastic. Educated consumers learn to precycle plastics once they "break the code," buying only those plastic food containers that are recyclable in their area.

PET: Polyethylene terephthalate, code #1, is the only plastic that can hold carbonated liquids. Most clear and green soda bottles, and plastic liquor bottles, are made of PET. Another clue to help you identify a container made of PET is that they have no seams, only a small raised dot or nipple (called a gate) in the center of the base.

All PET containers are recyclable; in some areas, however, you will have to remove the caps before recycling.

HDPE: High-density polyethylene, code #2, is a lightweight plastic, usually tough and colorful. You will find the #2 code designation on the bottom of milk jugs, detergent bottles, shampoos, some yogurt containers, juice bottles, and others. It is estimated that over 60 percent of plastic bottles are made with HDPE. The plastic grocery bags that "crinkle" are also HDPE material. HDPE is recyclable. In many areas you will be required to rinse out the bottle, and recyclers will often ask you to remove caps and "collars." Your children will develop a good "stomp" after mashing the milk jugs and attempting to shove them into your recycling bin.

PVC: Polyvinyl chloride, code #3 V, is recyclable in some areas, but it leaches vinyl chloride and is best avoided. It is still used as a food container for such products as cooking oil, water, and food "cling" wraps (the wraps with the blue tinge). Other PVC plastic products are garden hoses, credit cards, shower curtains, floor tiles, pipes, and mouthwash bottles.

LDPE: Low-density polyethylene, code #4, is usually the "shrink wrap" plastic used for packaging, dry-cleaning covers, sandwich bags, squeezable food and cosmetic containers, and soft, shiny grocery bags. This plastic is recyclable but the best advice is again to avoid and reuse as much as possible.

PP: Polypropylene, code #5, is rarely recycled. It is a light plastic that is used to make bottle caps, lids, cottage cheese tubs, and disposable diaper linings. It contains syrups and other products that need to be hot when they are poured into their container. Polypropylene has a very high heat resistance.

PS: Polystyrene, code #6, is a CFC-producing product, and is recyclable in some areas. PS is used to make bottles and pharmaceutical containers for salves and ointments, but it constitutes only 1 percent of all plastic bottles. Usually, PS is a foam formed into shipping chips, hot-food trays, and hot-liquid cups. Use your precycling skills to avoid polystyrene.

Plastics are still an environmental threat and generate some of the most contaminating hazardous waste materials during production. Continue to avoid plastics and recycle whatever you can.

▶ **5** If you remodel or renovate your home, consider the disposal of your building waste. Excess wood, steel products, paint cans, insulation, etc., all need to be properly disposed of. Plan to reuse construction waste. Before paying someone to haul the remaining waste to a landfill, contact a recycler. Check the phone directory under "Salvage Materials," "Used Lumber," "Restoration," "Building Materials," or check with your county public works department.

▶ **6** Reuse or recycle your old and worn tires. Retreading old tires is one of the most common forms of tire recycling; there is, however, an increasing market for "rubber crumbs" (shredded tires) which are added to asphalt pavement to increase its durability. Old tires can also be reused in the garden as planters, retaining walls, or hillside steps.

The best advice for tire owners is to precycle. Buy long-life tires, or keep them properly inflated and rotate them every 6,000 miles. For tire-recycling information in your state, consult the:

Directory of Scrap Tire Processors
Rubber Manufacturers Association
1400 K. St., N.W.
Washington, D.C. 20005
202-682-4800

▶ **7** Start a recycling program at work or school. Contact:

Keep America Beautiful
9 W. Broad St.
Stamford, CT 06902

World Resources Institute
1709 New York Ave., N.W., Suite 700
Washington, D.C. 20006

learning activities

▶ **1** *Recycle.* We've discussed all the ways you can recycle around your home. We all generate many different kinds of trash that can be recycled. What about the trash found in our public areas. Do you think that trash is recycled? Why not do it yourself?

- Organize your family, school, church group, or neighborhood to clean up a designated area every week. It could be the local park, beach, or picnic area. You choose.
- Make a concerted effort to stick to your schedule of tending the area you have chosen once a week, or even once a month. Pick up all the trash you find, recyclable or not. Have a contest to see who picks up the most in a day and reward that person with an "eco-prize." It could be a nature book or poster, a T-shirt from an environmental organization, anything you can think of. If you recycle the metal cans you find at a place that pays you for them, the proceeds from your collection can be used to buy the prize. Or you could save your earnings over the course of a year and do something really special with the money, like making your group a member of your favorite environmental organization, or adopting a whale or an acre of rain forest.

▶ **2** *Beautiful Junk.* Have the children collect some "junk" from around the house: toilet paper tubes, packaging chips, milk and egg cartons, shoe boxes, fabric and yarn remnants, old buttons, wood and wallpaper scraps, coat hangers, etc. Once the collection is established, the kids can decorate a box to hold it all. Whenever you hear the words "I'm bored," direct the children to the junk box and let them create a masterpiece. Glue, crayons, scissors, and imagination are all it takes. To trigger their creative talents suggest they make a bird feeder, board games, jewelry, a collage, mobiles, wind socks, boats, flower arrangements, flowerpots, drums, paper dolls, puppets, or masks.

▶ **3** *Make Your Own Paper.* Recycling paper will take on a whole new meaning once you do it yourself. You will need:

an old newspaper (comic strips will add some color)
water
a measuring cup
a three-inch-deep pan

window screen (enough to fit in the bottom of the pan)
a blender
scrape plastic or old plastic bag
heavy books

Begin by shredding two to three pages of newspaper. Place the bits of paper in the blender and add five cups of water. "Blend" the paper and water until it turns into pulp (and looks like very wet mashed potatoes).

While you are blending the paper, fill the pan with about an inch of water. Cut and fit the window screen to line the bottom of the pan.

When the pulp is blended, pour about a cupful into the pan of water and mix it.

Lift the screen from the pan (the pulp will be resting on top) and let the water drain.

Carefully place the screen and pulp on a piece of dry, opened-up newspaper. Close the paper. Place a piece of scrap plastic or an old plastic bag on top of the newspaper and stack four or five heavy books on top.

Check your recycled paper in a day or two, making sure it is dry before removing it from the screen. You and your child can now write a letter on it expressing your concerns for the environment.

▶ 4 *Conduct a Trash Analysis.* Most people throw away a lot of trash that could be reused. Make a list of all the items you can recycle and compost (i.e., glass, cans, newspapers, plastic, paper bags, cardboard, banana peels, apple cores). Keep a week-long trash inventory at home or at school, recording a tally of what went into the trash that could have been composted or recycled. Post the results of the tally and make suggestions if there are some trash habits that need to be changed.

Compost

Composting is an age-old natural process whereby organic matter is broken down biologically to produce a nutrient-rich material for soil enhancement. Composting your organic matter (in the form of food waste) at home introduces rich nutrients into the soil and can provide an excellent boost to your garden.

Community composting projects in which leaves, garden clippings, and Christmas trees from a number of households are gathered, have benefited many communities with beautiful, low-cost parklands and community gardens. Other forms of compost produce biogas, used as a source of energy. State-of-the-art municipal compost facilities can produce as much as 600 tons of finished compost a day. When this kind of high-tech waste reduction gets into full swing, the benefit to our land will be astounding. Not only will we be reducing our trash by 75 percent, we will be able to reclaim wastelands stripped of topsoil and reduce our dependence on chemical fertilizers for farming.

At home, composting is a means of turning kitchen and yard waste—75 percent of what we put out to be collected—into a nutrient-rich soil supplement for our yards and gardens. Grass clippings, coffee grounds, tea bags, food scraps, and eggshells are but a few of the organic compost materials we generally throw away. All you have to do is separate these materials in a compost heap outdoors and the benefits of your labor will be visible in the form of rich, organic soil and home waste reduction in a few short weeks.

make a difference!

▶ **1** Rather than using nonorganic fertilizers on your lawn and garden, find out if your community offers delivery of composted material or leaf mulch.

▶ **2** Experts estimate that Americans throw out 24 million tons of leaves, grass clippings, and other organic yard waste every year. It is unfortunate that people do not realize the value of their waste. Compost your yard waste or contact your local public works department to find out if they have a collection program for the community.

▶ **3** Compost your household organic waste and return the nourishing results back to the land. If you are concerned about rodents, investigate animal-proof compost bins.

learning activities

▶ **1** *Graveyard Garbage.* Words like "biodegradable," "organic," "compost," and "decompose" often confuse children. This simple experiment will be great fun for them and will help them to understand these basic concepts. You'll need:

"treasure"
Popsicle sticks
a pen
a shovel or trowel

Have the children find a few "treasures" that they would like to bury: a small plastic bag, piece of bread, soda bottle, tin can, old glove, piece of bark or wood chip.

Bury the items in holes in the backyard or garden and then mark them with Popsicle sticks to indicate their contents and the date they were buried.

Wait a few months and then unearth the items. What are the differences in level of decomposition? Compare the organic with the inorganic specimens. Attempt to explain the words *biodegrade, compost, decompose.* This visual experience will aid in the comprehension of important environmental concepts.

Rebury some of the items that did not react much to their underground experience (a tin can and old glove, for example), and check again in a year or two, just for the fun of it. Are there any changes this time?

▶ **2** *Build a Compost Pile.* Before you start outdoors, consider how you will collect the kitchen scraps indoors. A bucket with a lid is one of the best methods of collection. (An open container will attract fruit flies and, if left too long, will begin to smell—decomposing before your eyes.) Parents are often skeptical of compost heaps because of a fear of attracting rodents. If you do not have a rodent-hunting cat, be careful not to include any bones, meat, cheese, or grease in your compost. Using only vegetable scraps, grass, and garden clippings is the safest way of ensuring that your compost heap will remain free of rodents.

- Outdoors, you will need a pile of dry materials (dry leaves, grass clippings, straw, weeds) and a pile of fresh scraps (kitchen scraps and any fresh clippings). Avoid Bermuda grass and wild morning glory because their seeds may end up spreading to your garden once you have distributed the finished compost.

- Locate your compost heap in the shade, near the garden and a water supply. You will also need to enclose the heap. Some people buy compost containers. But you can also remove the bottom of an old tin garbage can and punch some holes in the sides for air, use wire mesh, or build a frame using wood or concrete blocks. To hold the heat which allows the organic matter to decompose, a compost pile should be at least four feet long, four feet wide, and three feet tall. A smaller pile lacks the volume required for rapid decomposition, but it will still work.

- When your site is ready you can begin the process. Start the pile with a layer of dry materials (about four inches high). Water the layer and pile on a few inches of wet scraps from the kitchen. Water each layer. You will not have a great compost pile until it reaches about three feet high. Cover the top with a thin layer of dirt to keep flies away. Add your new material as it is collected. Once the pile reaches a height of three feet you are ready to cover it and let it "cook." If the pile begins to smell, it is too wet, so make adjustments to what you add accordingly.

- If you have access to a long thermometer you can demonstrate to the children how the organic matter cooks from the inside out. The temperature of your pile will be several degrees higher inside.

- You will need to turn the compost periodically so air can circulate through it and help in the decomposition process. In three to five months the process should be complete. When the compost is dark and crumbly and has an earthy smell it is ready for use. You can add one to three inches to your garden to nourish the soil, or use it as potting soil for new plants. Many people try to keep two compost piles "cooking" so they have a constant supply to nourish their gardens.

- Something to remember: Keep the additions to your compost heap well-chopped and shredded. Larger pieces of matter take much longer to decompose.

Source Reduction

The key to success with any waste reduction plan is the reduction of waste at the source. Reduction of material and energy-use at the manufacturing stage (through improved product and packaging design), and more efficient production, are critical to reduction. Source reduction makes more efficient use of valuable resources and avoids disposal and pollution problems from the start.

We can include source reduction in our home waste reduction plan by precycling and buying from local manufacturers and farmers. Precycling means avoiding products with excess packaging or wasteful designs, disposables, and one-time-use products. By not purchasing these products we send a message to manufacturers to clean up their act and reconsider the impact their products have on the environment. Precycling is a skill developed by informed consumers who want to reduce waste at its source.

Recognizing hazardous waste and not purchasing hazardous-waste products is another highly beneficial form of source reduction. Fighting for legislation to eliminate such products and to spend money on the research and development of new, environmentally safe alternatives is an even further step for the motivated environmentalist.

make a difference!

▶ **1** Precycle by choosing products with the least amount of packaging. Dare yourself to leave overpackaged wrappings from vegetables and other products with the store manager in an effort to visually demonstrate your complaint.

▶ **2** Buy only what you need and use it all, or donate the "leftovers" to a friend.

▶ **3** Avoid bags. Make a commitment to always carry your own, and a promise never to accept or buy plastic ones regardless of their advertised value.

▶ **4** Do whatever you can at home, work, school, and business to reduce the tidal wave of trash.

▶ **5** Break the "clean machine" syndrome. Don't line the trash can, just wash it out when it becomes too dirty. Don't buy a dozen different hazardous household cleaning products—try the alternatives. Stop watching television commercials that attempt to convince you and your children that "Mr. Clean" and the Tidy Bowl man are supernatural agents required for good housekeeping.

▶ **6** Write or call companies that send unwanted junk mail and have your name removed from their mailings lists. Write to the company listed below and request that your name not be sold to other companies:

Mail Preference Service
Direct Marketing Association
11 West 42nd St.
P.O. Box 3861
New York, NY 10163-3861

▶ **7** Set aside a box for all your junk mail. When time permits, sit down with the kids and sort through the box. Make the necessary phone calls to eliminate your name from unwanted lists. Have the kids sort the paper into three recycling piles: newsprint, white paper, and colored paper. Tear out the plastic windows in the envelopes and recycle those too.

HAZARDOUS WASTE

What is toxic in your home? Many of the products we use for housework, gardening, home improvement, and car maintenance contain hazardous materials. They can endanger our health and that of our family—if not directly, then through the leachate materials left behind in landfills or toxic ash from incinerators. There is no escape from toxic materials other than to eliminate them at their source. Our greatest enemy is our own ignorance and fear. Knowing what is toxic in our homes and how to use it, store it, and dispose of it is essential to the protection of ourselves, our families, and our planet from harm.

How do you know if something is hazardous? The label tells it all. Look for warning words: "DANGER . . . WARNING . . . CAUTION . . . KEEP OUT OF REACH OF CHILDREN . . . POISON . . . IRRITANT . . . HARMFUL OR FATAL IF SWALLOWED . . . FLAMMABLE . . . COMBUSTIBLE . . . VOLATILE . . . CORROSIVE." All of these warning words indicate that the contents contain hazardous materials. You can protect your family from accidents by avoiding these materials, seeking alternatives, and accepting the fact that the effects of many of these materials is yet unknown.

Be a smart shopper. Read labels and choose the least toxic product available. Buy only as much as you need and will be able to use up in a short period. Select water-based products over solvent-based products like shoe polish, glue, and paint. Avoid aerosol sprays, choosing other methods of "product delivery." Most propellants contain petroleum distillate, toluene, chlorinated hydrocarbons, and ketones. These mist particles enter lungs, then the bloodstream, leaving carcinogenic ingredients in our bodies. Wear gloves and other protective gear to fully protect yourself against exposure to a hazardous material. And be especially careful not to mix products containing toxic ingredients.

If you have to store toxic household products, make sure their containers are tightly sealed and upright. Keep materials in their original containers and never rinse these containers or reuse them. It is a crime in the United States to throw hazardous materials in the trash, pour them down a sink, or wash them down a storm drain. Store household toxins away from food products and heat sources, and out of the reach of children. Separate flammables, corrosives, and poisons, and store them on separate shelves.

Recycle the hazardous waste if possible. Motor oil, transmission oil, antifreeze, and auto batteries all can be recycled at participating service stations and recycling centers. To dispose of any other toxic waste, contact your community household hazardous materials program for local disposal information. By simply tossing out an old flashlight battery or dumping ashes from the fireplace, we contribute to our hazardous waste problem. Educating ourselves and our children about these products is essential to our health and the health of our planet.

The materials listed below are considered household hazardous waste products. Understanding the proper form of their disposal is essential to protecting our land and waterways. In almost all cases, they are toxic, corrosive irritants that should be disposed of properly by the hazardous waste treatment plant in your area, and never in the weekly trash. The general rule of thumb is to make sure the contents of a container are completely used before disposing of it.

Abrasive cleaners or powders
Ammonia-based cleaners
Bleach cleaners
Disinfectants
Drain cleaners
Enamel or oil-based paints
Floor and furniture polish
Household batteries
Latex or water-based paints
Mothballs
Oven cleaners
Paint thinners and turpentine
Pesticides
Photographic chemicals
Pool chemicals
Rug and upholstery cleaners
Rust paints, wood preservatives, stains, finishes, and furniture
strippers
Toilet cleaners

make a difference!

▶ Make a commitment to dispose of leftover household toxins on designated community collection days (if they exist). Otherwise, contact your local hazardous waste program and find out how to properly dispose of the toxins.

flora
and fauna

Every creature is better alive than
dead—men, moose, and pine trees—and he
who understands it aright will rather preserve
it live rather than destroying it.

Henry David Thoreau

IN the Introduction to this book we frequently mentioned plants
and animals and the importance of our relationship as humans to
these different species. Please keep in mind that the word
"species"—often mistakenly assumed to mean only "animals"—is
used in reference to *all* living beings—a category which most def-
initely includes plants. How do plants (flora) and animals (fauna)
fit into our lives and the changing environmental picture? What is
their value to the human family? They can provide us with food,
medicine, industrial raw materials, pets, cultivated hobbies, and a
tonic for our stressed lives. Is that all? *Not at all.*

The preservation of all living things, or to use a phrase that is
becoming increasingly common, "biological diversity" (or "biodi-

versity," if we want to save a few syllables), is critical to the survival of the planet. Biodiversity is that glorious array of all living things that inhabit the Earth: every plant, bird, insect, fish, animal, human being, and the place (or habitat) each needs to survive. All have a definite place and function on this planet. The loss or disruption of the life of one causes a chain reaction throughout the lives and existence of various others. Biodiversity, because of that multitude of functions, is the most important natural resource we have. It is what will ensure that our children and our children's children will inherit and be able to maintain a decent quality of life. For each species that is driven to extinction, the foundation of earthly existence for all other species is weakened. Why?

• A generous half of all the medicines we have to cure our ailments comes from plants, and a smaller percentage from less visible animals such as worms, amphibians, insects, fish, and reptiles. In their myriad evolutions, these species have developed chemical processes for dealing with the forces in their lives—illness, self-defense, birth, digestion, attracting mates, etc.—under a multitude of ever-changing conditions. These same evolutionary forces and changing conditions occur among the human family as well, though obviously under different circumstances.

Among our plant- and animal-derived medicines are drugs used to control heart disease and treat various forms of cancer. Even penicillin, the most common antibiotic drug used to treat infections, comes from a plant fungus. With all the species yet to be discovered, we may be able to find treatments and cures for other life-threatening ailments.

• Our food supply, and that of animals as well, is dependent on a vast array of other plant and animal species, and ultimately on the survival of those species' wild cousins. Today, our agricultural practices depend on relatively few domesticated species. This small number provides a very narrow base in the event of a disaster—a disease or blight that may wipe out a particular crop, for example. Remember the potato famine of the nineteenth century? One of the best defenses against the recurrence of such an event is the blending of vulnerable domestic species with hardier wild versions. An infusion of stronger genes helps protect species from certain diseases. Much research is being applied to this kind of crop enhancement. Again, there may be undiscovered species available to aid in that research.

• Plants and animals provide natural flood-pest-control services, contribute to soil productivity, and act as waste decomposers. Green leaves absorb the heat-absorbing gas carbon dioxide and release oxygen. The root systems of plants along with assorted worms, insects, and fungi, control stream flows and groundwater levels, help recycle soil minerals, and clean pollutants from surface water. Insects, birds, and bats are valuable seed pollinators and dispensers.

• What about the delight other living things give to human beings? How would we feel in the absence of beautiful trees and flowers, or the animals that remind us of a world other than our concrete buildings and the noisy, frantic existences that go with them?

issue

The preservation of biodiversity is being severely threatened for one primary reason—the disappearance of natural habitats. The lands species need to survive are being destroyed; all kinds of habitats for all kinds of species. Our burgeoning population, sprawling development, irresponsible agricultural practices, and disregard for the importance of other creatures on the Earth have already led to severe habitat devastation. Many believe that this situation is indeed the most desperate of all the environmental ills we face.

Like humans, every species must have a home in a suitable climate with enough food and water, clean air (or water, for fish) to breathe, and enough protection from danger to allow them to reproduce. People threaten these basic needs in several ways: We pollute the air and water so that plants and animals can no longer live in areas where they may have lived for centuries; we turn wild areas into buildings, factories, and houses; we hunt and fish too much and do not allow the species enough time to reproduce; and we bring new species into an area where they may be stronger than the native species, forcing the native species to look for other places to live.

Roughly 1.5 million plant and animal species have been identified and named. Scientists believe there are 20 to 30 million more, but that we are losing three to five of them per day to extinction. At the current rate of habitat destruction, we could see that figure rise to over a hundred species *per day* by the year 2000—a hundred species that may hold the key to a cure for AIDS, cancer, diabetes, and other serious diseases. We may even be able to find a cure for the common cold in the leaf of some yet-to-be-discovered plant. But that will not be possible if we destroy its chances for survival before we have had time to locate it.

Human survival depends on the survival of all other species. Our peaceful and supportive coexistence encourages a balance if we are not to lose our food supply, medicines, clean air, and last, but not least, natural beauty.

HOW DO VARIOUS SPECIES HELP US?

To give you and your child some insight into the debt we owe the natural world for our foods and medicines, we have listed below a number of the scientific uses which the world's plant and animal species provide for us. All of these exciting discoveries have come about within the last ten years. Think about the great loss to all of us if even one of these species were to become extinct. Think about the possibilities of thousands of similar exciting discoveries yet to be made with species we already know about, and the discoveries possible with species not yet known. Share these with your children—kids just love these "believe it or not" kinds of stories.

- The kouprey, a wild ox native to Cambodia, is immune to rinderpest, one of the leading killers of domestic cattle. Scientists had hoped to breed the kouprey with domestic cattle in order to genetically pass on the rinderpest immunity. Unfortunately, the kouprey may be extinct.
- Milkweed plants convert sunlight into the same hydrocarbons found in petroleum. Scientists can extract this petroleum and other synthetic fuels from the plants.

- Found in the Mexican desert, the guayule plant is a hardy species requiring very little water. It can be harvested two to three years after planting and is 10 to 20 percent rubber by weight. A couple of manufacturers are now testing tires made of guayule for potential markets.
- Scientists are studying a small Australian frog that gives birth through its mouth. The purpose of the study is to discover how the frog "turns off" the hydrochloric acid enzymes in the stomach to allow birth to take place. The findings of this study may lead to a drug which can stop the flow of acid in human stomachs and allow ulcers to heal naturally, or prevent them in the first place.
- An ancient grain called amaranth, once a staple of the Aztec culture, contains an amino acid not found in any other grain. A diet containing amaranth and other grains such as wheat, rice, and corn could provide a complete protein without adding milk or other expensive animal proteins. Because it grows in semiarid conditions, the amaranth could be a viable answer to the hunger problems of certain less developed countries.
- Evening primrose seeds contain an oil rich in a particular acid that scientists believe may control heart disease and arthritis, among other illnesses.
- Extracts from cucumber skins and bay leaves are being synthesized to produce effective cockroach repellents.
- Scientists are conducting experiments on flatworms because of their ability to repair severed nerves. It is hoped that we can adapt some of their abilities to aid in human nerve repair.
- A particular species of potato grown in Bolivia has glue-tipped hairs on its leaves, stems, and sprouts which trap insects that damage the potato plant. Scientists hope to develop the plant for agricultural pest-control purposes, as an alternative to harmful chemical insecticides.
- The substance that mussels use to attach themselves to rocks is being studied as a possible "super glue" that doctors could use for fusing broken bones and/or lacerated soft tissue.
- The African elephant trunk fish is being used in several

European cities to test the quality of their drinking water. Under normal conditions these fish emit hundreds of electrical signals to mark their territory. Small amounts of pollution cause the fish to decrease the number of signals they send out. This allows the water to be constantly monitored for pollution levels.

- Cyclosporin A is a drug used to prevent the body from rejecting transplanted organs. It is derived from two strains of fungi first discovered in a Wisconsin soil sample.
- Experiments conducted with the oil from orange peels reveal that it can kill pests such as fleas, wasps, and flies, without harming humans, other animals, or the environment.
- A microscopic worm called the roundworm attacks termites in their larval stages. Because it is not harmful to humans, pets, or plants, it is being considered as a domestic solution to household termite problems.
- A substance isolated from the skin of a lizard has been determined to be as effective as morphine in relieving pain in humans.
- A particular tree fungus may hold part of the solution to our toxic waste problems. The fungus degrades pesticides and other toxic substances into harmless chemicals.
- A native tree of Asia, the neem, has been discovered to be a powerful source for a new insecticide. Extracts from the neem tree, sprayed on leaves or applied to the soil, can repel six species of cockroaches as well as 80 percent of other insects.
- *Lippis dulcis*, a plant that grows in Latin America, has leaves and flowers that are 1,000 times sweeter than sucrose. The derivative is nontoxic, has no adverse effects, and very few calories.
- Believed to have certain properties that bolster the immune system, the black bean is being studied as a possible cure for AIDS and cancer.
- The federally protected desert pupfish is being studied for its resistance to calcium salts, a well-known cause of kidney failure in adults. If we discover what protects the pupfish,

scientists may be able to develop a treatment for humans.
• Painkillers and anti-inflammatory drugs are being extracted from a soft Caribbean coral called "sea whip." The
coral is non-narcotic and, as a result, nonaddictive.

These are but a few examples of the fascinating ways in which
plants and animals make our human existence easier. We owe it to
ourselves to ensure their existence.

make a difference!

▶ **1** Make an effort to investigate local species which may be
threatened with extinction and try to involve your child in the
rehabilitation process. The National Wildlife Federation publishes
a list of endangered species which you can use as a reference.

▶ **2** Support your local zoos, aquariums, and botanical gardens.
Species are not held in captivity for public enjoyment alone. Among
other things, they allow us to study ways of ensuring the existence
of various species well into the future. Captive breeding programs
are conducted to ensure population growth for many threatened
animals. Many programs breed endangered species and then return them to their natural habitat.

▶ **3** Adopt an animal. Many zoos have programs which for a donation allow you to "adopt" an animal. Adoptions usually begin at
$15 but can climb into the thousands depending on the animal you
choose to adopt. This would make a great school or class project.
For more expensive adoptions, creative fund-raising ideas can be
used to fund the project. To learn more about animal adoption,
contact the American Association of Zoological Parks (address in
Chapter 9).

▶ **4** Visit and support nature parks and preserves. The Nature
Conservancy, an international membership organization which
owns the largest private preserve system in the world, has sanc-
tuaries in all fifty states. (See Chapter 9 for address and telephone
information.)

▶ **5** Encourage Congress to support and enforce the Endangered
Species Act and other legislation designed to protect threatened
species and ecosystems. (See Appendix 3 for Effective Letter Writing.)

▶ **6** Plant trees. This is one of the easiest, most enjoyable, and interesting projects you and your family can undertake.

- Try to plant trees on the south or southeast side of your house. This will help cut air-conditioning costs by 10 to 50 percent in the summer. Shade from the trees will keep the hot sun from overheating your house.
- Trees use carbon dioxide to grow. Planting them can help cut the amount of harmful carbon dioxide emissions from cars and other machines.
- Trees bearing treats like fruits and nuts make a wonderful addition to the neighborhood.

▶ **7** Join or form a neighborhood or block association, and make tree planting one of your neighborhood or block improvement projects. Make your child a part of these projects.

▶ **8** Form a similar organization to plant trees at your neighborhood schools. This is an excellent undertaking for parent-teacher associations.

▶ **9** When it is safe to do so, leave dead tree limbs undisturbed. They provide shelter for certain birds and provide food for others.

▶ **10** Allow annual and perennial plants to go to seed before cutting them back. These too will provide food and shelter for birds.

▶ **11** Plant pest-resistant plant species. This will help cut down on the amount of pesticides that may be required to maintain your garden and that will eventually leach into the groundwater.

▶ **12** Plant trees and shrubs that attract birds. Native fruit trees and seed-bearing bushes provide food for hungry birds.

▶ **13** Investigate natural pest-control methods. Did you know that there are over thirty-five bird species that feed on the pesky gypsy moth? Attracting these birds to your yard with food and by cultivating certain plant species could significantly reduce your need for pesticides.

▶ **14** Have you ever thought about using a live tree to decorate your home during the Christmas season? Millions of trees are cut down each year. The day after Christmas, countless trees lie unbought and wasted in the sales lots—trees that should never have been cut down. You can buy a live tree and leave it in a pot for use the next year, or plant it in your yard and buy another live tree the following year.

▶ **15** Planting should not be thought of as a strictly outdoor activity. You can grow all sorts of plants indoors from seeds or seedlings. To expand your recycling program, use old food containers to start plants. Old yogurt cups make excellent starter pots. Coffee cans and milk jugs (after cutting a third off the top) make great planters. Kids will enjoy decorating them with stickers and colored paper.

▶ **16** Don't buy any products made from endangered species. Many of them are listed in Chapter 8.

▶ **17** Don't buy helium-filled balloons. Many of these balloons when released, accidentally or not, end up in areas where wildlife, especially marine life, are likely to come in contact with them. In fact, sometimes they are mistaken for food and can kill the creatures that eat them.

▶ **18** Animals can be hurt by the garbage you throw away. They will sometimes eat litter that they think is food, or become trapped in containers, etc. The Defenders of Wildlife has a booklet called *Deadly Throwaways* that will provide you with more information. (See Chapter 9 for address and telephone information.)

▶ **19** Snip six-pack rings from soda and beer cans before disposing of them. They can otherwise make their way into the ocean and harm marine life. Shorebirds and fish sometimes get their necks caught in rings floating in the water.

learning activities

▶ **1** Why not build your own backyard habitat? It will enable you to provide a home for many plants and animals as well as observe how their lives interact with one another. Consider creating a pond. Here's how.

• You will need the following materials:

a shovel
a large sheet of durable plastic
a tarp or other sturdy material
large stones
straw
pond vegetation (a local plant store should have plants that are indigenous to your area)
water—rainwater is best for this project
a bucket of water, mud, and weeds from another pond (this

bucket, containing many tiny plant creatures, will help
populate your pond environment)

Locate your pond away from any large trees, as falling
autumn leaves can pose a problem. Try to place it near a
flower bed, or preferably a rock garden. This will offer toads
and frogs protection when they need it.

Dig a hole at least six feet across and two feet deep. The
sides should have a gentle slope with several shelves placed
at different levels. This, too, will help animals to get in and
out of the pond, and provide growing space for vegetation as
well.

Remove all large stones and sticks and cover the bottom of
the hole with a tarp or other sturdy material to prevent the
plastic from being punctured.

Thoroughly clean any possible chemical residue from the
plastic and lay it in the hole, securing it along the edges
with heavy stones.

Add some of the dug-up earth and straw to the hole before
filling it with water. Avoid filling it to the top; leave at least
four or five inches to prevent possible overflow from rain.

Add your bucket of organic goodies from the other pond. It
will be full of plants, seeds, and animals that will help establish your pond.

Place your purchased plants in the pond. Try to keep them
in some sort of container that will allow for growth and easy
arrangement in the water. Secure the containers with
stones.

Arrange some large stones around the water's edge so that
animals can get in and out.

There is no need to buy any animals. Eventually animals
will find the pond on their own. Part of the fun is watching
for them. Be patient. It may take some time.

Should the pond become murky, add a supply of pond
snails. They eat the tiny algae that can often cloud your
pond.

▶ **2** Go out and see how may habitats you can identify in your own
neighborhood. Remember, even something as small as an anthill

qualifies as a habitat. Any place that an animal, a bird, an insect, or a person calls "home" is a habitat.

▶ **3** Plant trees! Trees recycle water, oxygen, and carbon dioxide, all of which help to reduce soil erosion, flooding, and air pollution. They provide us with paper, fruit and nuts, rubber, wood, fibers, homes for birds and animals, and sturdy limbs for kids to climb. It is perhaps the easiest contribution you can make to help clean up the environment.

- Plant one for each member of the family. Care for them as you would any other "pet." After all, they are living things and require care and nurturing as well.

▶ **4** Install a bird feeder in your yard. Build your own—a great family project—or buy a commercially manufactured product. Not only will you be amazed at how many different species appear, you'll be helping your bird friends to survive, especially during the cold winter months.

- Don't throw away stale bread or crackers. These make a great breakfast treat for birds. Sprinkle crumbs made from stale bread around your yard before you go off to work or school in the morning.
- Keep a journal of all the various species that come to your yard to feed.

▶ **5** Provide a birdbath for the birds that visit your yard. Use a container with an edge on it so the birds have a place to rest while they drink. The container should be nonmetal, as that will become either too hot or too cold depending on the season. For help with this, contact the National Audubon Society. (See Chapter 10.)

▶ **6** For $5.00, the National Wildlife Federation will show you how to turn your backyard into a wildlife habitat. If you draw a plan and submit it back to the organization, it will be reviewed; if it is accepted, you will be awarded a certificate recognizing that yours is an official Backyard Wildlife Habitat.

RAIN FORESTS

Nowhere on Earth, except in tropical coral reefs, is life more abundant or diverse than in the tropical rain forests. And nowhere, unfortunately, is this life more threatened or under attack.

There are more plant species in the rain forests of the tiny country of Panama than are found on the entire continent of Europe. Nearly 1,500 species of birds—16 percent of the world total—are found in Indonesian rain forests. A single river in Brazil is home to more kinds of fish than are found in all U.S. rivers combined. Sixty to eighty species of trees live in one acre of rain forest alone, in contrast to the twenty-five species per acre found in the lushest forests of the United States. There are thousands of equally startling statistics.

Rain forests also have a critical impact on global weather patterns. These lush areas absorb enormous quantities of solar energy, thus affecting wind and rainfall patterns around the world. The huge amounts of carbon dioxide contained in rain forest vegetation and released during deforestation contribute significantly to the "global warming" crisis—what we've come to know as the "greenhouse effect." Rain forests also help to prevent soil erosion in coastal areas which could be severely damaged by flooding and heavy winds. And yet we witness the daily destruction of these wonderlands at the shocking rate of over 32 million acres per year—*sixty-seven acres each minute*. With this level of habitat destruction comes the loss of untold species and the displacement of indigenous peoples, the human occupants of the rain forests. Without a suitable home, survival is severely jeopardized for all.

Great expanses of tropical rain forest grow around the equator through Central and South America, Central Africa, Southeast Asia, northern Australasia, and even in Hawaii and Alaska. All of them are similarly structured. There are five main layers, each with its own unique flora and fauna.

Emergent Layer
The tallest trees, some of them as high as 160 feet or more, occupy the top layer. It is from here—30 to 50 feet above the layer below— that eagles and other raptors (birds of prey) observe the animals they feed on in the lower levels.

Canopy
The canopy is considered the roof of the rain forest, and its most luxuriant layer. Rising 100 to 130 feet above the ground floor (herb layer), it is a thick intertwining of tree leaves and branches. The crowns of the trees are typically 3 feet apart to prevent wind dam-

age and hungry tree-eaters (caterpillars, etc.) from climbing from one tree to the next. Most of the rain forest plants and animals occupy this layer, where the sunshine is plentiful.

Understory
The tops of smaller trees make up this lower and less dense layer of vegetation. In the understory, palms and younger trees struggle to reach the sun. Various monkey species live here.

Shrub Layer
The growth of this layer's flora depends heavily on the sunlight that penetrates the upper layers—the more there is, the more quickly and densely the plant species will grow.

Herb Layer
Composed of ferns and herbs, this is the undergrowth of the rain forest. The area is home to the many insects that inhabit the rain forest.

issue
Economics plays a large role in the complex problem of tropical deforestation. Agriculture, logging, mining, and ranching—pursuits that provide short-term income for the people involved—contribute extensively to the problem. The forests must be cleared to make way for these activities. After a relatively few years the land, characterized by soil that is fertile *only* when supported by tropical forest vegetation, becomes barren—unable to support the very practices for which it was altered. Here is a brief explanation for why this occurs.

The floor of the rain forest is covered with several inches of fallen leaves. The decomposed organic material from the leaves is recycled very quickly: Minerals are transferred directly to the shallow root systems of the tropical trees and plants. The process works so efficiently that lower soil layers contain almost no minerals at all. All of them are stored in the vegetation itself.

The destruction of the forest causes the abundance of minerals to be lost, turned to ash. Root systems are destroyed and the resulting ash and topsoil are washed away. The soil that remains, because all minerals have been destroyed, is infertile, and the once lush rain forest is reduced to a barren wasteland. Any agricultural crops planted last two or three years at the most, after which time all the trace minerals are used up and the crops fail.

Another cause of deforestation is the gathering of wood for fuel. Many people living inside the rain forests depend exclusively on wood for cooking and heating fuel. When wood becomes unavailable, cow dung is used, depriving the soil of a valuable source of fertilizer. This excessive use of resources poses yet another serious problem.

The key, then, is to encourage the sustainable development of the many crops already produced by the rain forest. In effect, through bolstered consumer interest, forest dwellers and local business people should be encouraged to extract and sell renewable resources that will ensure the future survival of these forests.

Indigenous Peoples

A sad footnote to the destruction of tropical rain forests, and one which is sometimes lost in the overall discussion, is the displacement of indigenous peoples, those native tribes that have inhabited the forests for centuries.

As rain forests are destroyed, so are the homes and cultures of the tribes. They have little choice but to enter the cities, where they live in shameful poverty because they do not have adequate skills to exist in an urban environment. In the worst-case scenario, they slip into extinction and are lost forever. With them goes their knowledge of the secrets of the rain forest.

There are over 140 million people who inhabit the world's rain forests. A large percentage of them are indigenous tribal people. There are more than one thousand tribes that survive in rain forests around the world, and many of them are threatened. These cultures have much to teach western "civilization." Centuries of forest habitation have taught them about the plants that have special medicinal properties, and crops that can be sources of food. The Hanunóo people of the Philippines, for example, produce 430 rain forest crops.

make a difference!

▶ 1 Avoid buying shoes from Latin America. Leather is a by-product of cattle ranching, an activity responsible for the destruction of millions of acres of rain forest.

▶ **2** Avoid purchasing products made from tropical woods such as mahogany, teak, and rosewood. Obviously, trees need to be cut down to provide this wood.

▶ **3** Support products that sustain the rain forest. Tropical fruits, vegetables, rubber, etc., can be harvested safely and thereby encourage the care and maintenance of the rain forest. There are a number of companies that are actively incorporating rain forest products into their own goods—The Body Shop (an international cosmetic chain) uses rain forest plants in the production of its cosmetics, for example, and rain forest nuts are used in Ben and Jerry's ice cream.

▶ **4** Read books about the rain forest to your children and give them books they can read themselves. (A list of these books can be found in Chapter 9.)

▶ **5** Play tapes of rain forest "sounds" and let your child imaginatively experience the animals of the rain forest. An excellent tape called "Amazon Days, Amazon Nights" can be purchased from the National Resources Defense Council (you'll find the address and telephone number in Chapter 9). It is accompanied by notes identifying all the animals on the tape.

▶ **6** As an alternative gift idea (or for any other time), consider "adopting" an acre of rain forest. The Nature Conservancy offers such a program. For a $30 contribution, you can adopt an acre of rain forest in Latin America. Each adoption includes an honorary land deed, periodic updates on the particular adopt-an-acre projects (these vary as projects are completed), and membership in the Conservancy. The contributions are used to fund the acquisition of various tracts of rain forest through TNC's partner conservation organizations in Latin America, and to manage these areas once they have become parks.

learning activities

▶ **1** Build your own miniature rain forest. You and your kids can create (almost) a rain forest environment in a fish tank. You'll need:

gravel
charcoal
fish tank
rich compost

small stones
exotic plants

Place a layer of gravel and charcoal at the bottom of a fish tank.
Place a layer of rich compost over the first layer.
Shape the ground with an arrangement of small stones pressed into and under the compost.
Dampen the compost by sprinkling with water and follow by planting a few exotic plants. Your local plant store can help you with the most suitable species. Make sure the plants are not too close together. They need room to grow.
Replace the glass top and keep the tank in a warm, well-lit spot, but out of the direct sunshine.

The air will remain moist as the water is continually recycled between the compost, plants, and air in the tank. All you need to do is add a little water every few months and you'll have your very own rain forest.
▶ 2 Visit museums that have re-created rain forest environments. You'll get a good feel for the type of climate and vegetation that characterize rain forests.

ENVIRONMENTAL TERRORISM

Adding to the problems human ignorance and lack of attention have wreaked on the planet, is the terrifying threat of environmental terrorism—acts intentionally perpetrated against the environment to cause destruction, or resulting inadvertently from active warfare. We witnessed this outrage all too clearly during the recent war in the Middle East.
War has traditionally played a role in environmental degradation. Bombs cannot be dropped and tanks cannot be driven without causing severe damage to the landscape and the plants and animals that live within it. We have seen this happen again and again throughout history. No stand of trees, no rice paddy or beach can stand up to the violence of war and not incur some level of damage, permanent or otherwise.

The Persian Gulf Disaster

With the war in the Persian Gulf, a new form of damage to the environment has presented itself: outright destruction of the environment for political purposes. The facts are not all in yet, but it is believed that the acts of terrorism inflicted on the region could amount to the worst man-made environmental disaster in history.

Oil Spills

As an ecosystem, the Persian Gulf area is already in serious trouble. Years of oil tankers passing through the Gulf and spilling their cargo in varying degrees have left the beaches and waters dirty with residue. During the Iran–Iraq war, a spill at Norwuz created an oil slick that was over six hundred miles long—the full length of the Gulf. That eight-year war saw a 50 percent increase in Gulf oil spills due to increased traffic and the damage inflicted on tankers by mines. The January 1991 crisis has already resulted in a spill of major proportions, the largest in history. It could exceed by a hundredfold the damage caused by the 1989 *Exxon Valdez* spill.

The toxins released in a spill of this magnitude—not only carcinogenic hydrocarbons, but heavy metals such as lead, mercury, and arsenic—result in the death of birds, finfish and shellfish, dolphins, sea turtles, snakes, and marine plant life. The devastation inflicted on the food chain and the subsequent loss of productivity (continued healthy breeding of species) is set in motion. Recovery is painstakingly slow, though with a spill of this size the jury is still out as to whether recovery is even possible. Cleaning up this kind of intentional disaster will put the knowledge of many scientists to the test for many years to come.

Oil Well Fires

Not only was oil deliberately released into the environment by men dependent upon that ecosystem for food and water, but the lunacy persisted and oil wells and storage tanks were set ablaze as well. More of this kind of sabotage can be expected, since oil is considered a powerful pawn in the war among nations.

Chemical/Biological Weapons Plant Destruction

Great fears arise at the very thought of using chemical and biological weapons as war tactics. But what about the possibility of those toxins (chemical) and diseases (biological) being released into the air as a result of air and ground attacks? Could the residues released as a result of damage to holding tanks persist in the atmosphere? On the ground? It is generally believed that oil-based chemicals like mustard gas (a known carcinogen, or cancer-causing agent, used recently in the Iran-Iraq war) have a longer life than some of the other chemical weapons, inviting persistent problems well into the next century.

Pollution and the Military Machine

Military installations are notorious for their liberal use of fossil fuels in the form of gasoline, kerosene (as jet fuel), and others. The quantities consumed are significant enough during peacetime, but during wartime the quantities reach enormous proportions, greatly affecting supplies and necessitating increased extraction.

The tragic brutalizing of the Earth and her inhabitants in a time of war is inexcusable. The blatant destruction of the animals, plants, and people the Earth supports is unforgivable. What are routinely considered as political maneuverings to elicit response are criminal acts that threaten the existence of everyone, every living being, not just those on the *other* side of the line. Ironically, the very war- and weapons-technology that is supposed to protect us is now capable of making the Earth we all share totally uninhabitable.

learning activities

▶ 1 Have your child research the flora and fauna that suffers the most from an oil spill in a particular part of the world. Encourage them to join organizations like the Center for Marine Conservation that actively work to help these species (see Chapter 9 for address and telephone information).

▶ 2 Pull out the family atlas and discuss where these events are occurring. Show them the marine areas that can be affected by oil spills.

environmentally responsible products

There is sufficiency in the world for man's need but not for man's greed.

Gandhi

OURS is a consumer-oriented society. Each year we spend billions of dollars on goods and services in an attempt to beautify, simplify, and generally elevate the quality of our lives. Consumption of one sort or another is a daily fact of life. We consume not only in direct ways, as with food and water, but in an indirect way as well. Everything we buy, use, or discard during the day involves the extraction of raw materials, energy consumption for manufacture and distribution, and land use for its inevitable disposal. Needless to say, we take this consumption for granted. We work, we earn, we buy, we consume.

But everything we buy has some sort of environmental impact. Products do not simply appear on our market shelves. They go through lengthy, energy-intensive processes to reach us.

From raw material, to energy consumption, to production, to processing, to human acquisition, to landfills, the implications of product consumption are numerous. Each of these steps contributes to the pollution and decimation of our environment. Our desire for "more" and "better" takes its expensive toll in terms of cost both to the consumer and the environment.

issue

The raw materials needed to produce goods are extracted from the Earth and require enormous quantities of energy to transform them into consumer goods. These, in turn, again use enormous amounts of energy in the packaging and distribution phases. We then buy them, use what we want, and discard the unused portions, resulting in untold amounts of waste.

This chapter focuses on our role and responsibility as consumers—individuals who, by virtue of our buying power, can influence the choices made available to us by manufacturers—and on safe, environmentally sound choices that interfere as little as possible with the Earth's natural processes. People are finally reacting to the expense of "production," and beginning to understand that our consumption of and reliance on modern innovations has not made our lives any easier, and in fact often makes them much more complicated. Many people are now willing to begin simplifying their lives to accommodate a more sensible, environmentally friendly consumption. This "green consumerism" is a rapidly growing practice among concerned people and will be outlined in the following pages.

Manufacturers have heard this new consumer cry and are acting quickly to respond to it. Unfortunately, many of their product "responses" are misrepresentations of reality, false attempts to appeal to our consciences. Packaging, for instance, is often redesigned to attract our environmental conscience, but, in fact, only catchy jargon is used. The contents sadly lack any resemblance to a responsible alternative.

What we will focus on in the following pages are those companies that are devoted to research, manufacturing practices, and product distribution practices that do not disrupt the balance between our need and desire for certain products, and Mother Earth—or at least not as badly as some others do. Because the confusion between those that do and those that do not is significant, we will try to shed some light on this for you.

DEVELOPING "GREEN HABITS"

Consider the following three themes, a cyclical thought process you can use when shopping and one that may help you respond to the need for buying "green" and adopting green habits.

▶ 1 Less is best—simplify your life. Use one all-purpose cleaning product as opposed to several to do the same task.
▶ 2 Does the product have an "afterlife" other than ending up in a landfill? Are you committed to following through with the reuse and recycling of the product?
▶ 3 Is the product made of natural ingredients or synthetic and possibly planet-threatening chemical compounds? Are there any alternative choices?

Remembering these three concepts is a good way to initiate important changes in your buying habits.

As you practice this thought process you will gradually discover that the changes are being made in your consciousness. You may notice that "green thinking" requires concerted effort in the beginning, but it will eventually become easier as you learn which products are more suitable than others, and which are right for your lifestyle. After some time, look back on your old consumer habits and pat yourself on the back! You have probably helped to prevent millions of tons of carbon dioxide from entering the atmosphere, saved habitats and the wildlife that inhabits them, even reduced toxic waste emission in your community. The greatest benefit of all is the subtle influence you will have on your family and friends. Without preaching, bragging, or ruling with an iron hand you will be contributing in some way to positive social change. Your children, after some possible initial squawks, will take for granted the products you use and the simpler way of life they entail. They will grow up to become educated consumers, and not think twice about supporting the unnecessary frills that you once could not imagine life without.

Right now we are riding the crest of a wave called "green consumerism." This mood has resulted in environmental advertising—a big-business response to our desire to preserve the planet.

As a result, consumer groups and for-profit organizations are searching for some sort of distinguishing trademark or logo to identify "green" products and help clear up some of the confusion and misrepresentation. Such a logo will also help children to identify incorrect products. One group is proposing a green cross, much like the "Good Housekeeping Seal of Approval," to help consumers identify Earth-conscious products. Nevertheless, one has to ask what defines an "Earth-conscious" product? Who sets the regulations? Who is benefiting from this identification program? What is the bottom line?

You are the bottom line. You will have to continually educate yourself on this subject, stick to the philosophy that less is best, and become a consumer advocate willing to fight for clear, straightforward advertising and to cut off violators at their source—through boycotts and letter-writing campaigns.

To further illustrate the confusion facing well-intentioned consumers, the following is a selection of frequently used eco-advertising terms and their rather vague meanings.

Nontoxic: There is no legal definition for this term. It implies, however, that the product will not harm or poison you. This misleading term does not take into account the harmful effects the product may have on children, plant, or animal life. For example, many children have suffered from painful stomachaches after chewing on "nontoxic" crayons. One representative of the National Poison Control Center in Washington, D.C., suggested that nontoxic simply alleges that a human being will not die from using the product. That's not necessarily how we react to the words nontoxic, is it?

Biodegradable: Everything will biodegrade eventually, though it could take anywhere from two weeks to two million years. Quite a spread. To date, there is no law defining an appropriate time frame for the biodegradation of a product. Manufacturers have been known to use this word as an environmental buzzword to entice consumers. "Biodegradable" suggests a solution to our waste management crisis regardless of whether or not a product contains chemicals that may harm groundwater supplies if they do biodegrade. Use caution whenever you see a product being advertised as biodegradable.

Natural: Lead is natural, carbon dioxide is natural, gas, coal, and oil are natural. Again there is no legal definition to set a limit on how far advertisers can go with the use of this word and its implication.

Cruelty-free: This suggests that the product was not tested on animals and will not hurt animals, but it does not mean that it won't hurt the planet in some way. Oil companies in general have greatly decreased their animal testing and some of their products are "cruelty-free." Nonetheless, oil companies, as we all know, commit some of the worst crimes against the environment.

Recyclable: Through the advances of modern technology, anything is recyclable. However, the expense and energy needed to recycle some products is often a violation of its resource-saving intent. Aseptic juice boxes are a perfect example of this advertising gimmick. There are very few places in the United States that recycle these energy-intensive little boxes. They are composed of various layers of paper, polyethylene, and foil, making them a complicated package to recycle. A can or bottle of juice that is easily recyclable would be a better choice than buying juice boxes.

Ozone safe: Many manufacturers of aerosols and pump sprays lure you into purchasing their products because they do not contain CFCs. Nonetheless, they release chemicals into the air that end up in our lungs and are a waste management concern. Alternative delivery systems such as creams, roll-ons, or sticks are always the best choice. For information regarding the undesirable ingredients to look for on aerosol can labels, contact:

The National Toxic Campaign
37 Temple Pl., 4th Fl.
Boston, MA 02111

High octane: Choosing a high-octane gas is more expensive and rarely required for most cars. The aromatic hydrocarbons— including benzene, toluene, and xylene—used to boost octane levels in gas are all hazardous pollutants. Repeated inhalation of benzene vapors has been associated with various fatal blood diseases such as aplastic anemia and leukemia.

Made from recycled materials: The difficulty here is in determining whether the product is made from 10 percent or 100 percent recycled material. There is no minimum amount of recycled material needed to state this claim. However, keep in mind that *something* recycled is always better than *nothing* recycled.

Environmentally friendly, environmentally safe, green: In terms of reality, these claims and others like them are meaningless. They are simply used to lure you or catch your eye and sell you the product. Though such labeling is often used with good intentions, *all products have some impact on the environment.* It will be up to you as a consumer to read labels and decide for yourself if you need the product, and then to assess what kind of impact it may have on the Earth.

Despite all the advertising gimmicks, some products are a better choice than others. For example, if you must use paper towels, choose ones made from recycled paper and preferably not packaged in plastic. By using recycled products you are helping to increase the demand for them, which will eventually lead to lower prices and decreased energy use.

Today's ecoeconomists are suggesting that we look at the *entire lifecycle* of a product before determining whether it is, in fact, a worthwhile choice. For example, a regular roll of bleached paper towels made of virgin paper and packaged in plastic, but with a "recycled cardboard tube," is not a sensible choice. Bleached paper contributes to water pollution and leaches dioxins into our bodies. Trees are destroyed to make this paper. Air and land are polluted by the high-energy and landfill waste that is associated with paper towels. The fact that the product's cardboard tube is made from recycled paper is rather insignificant in light of the other environmental factors.

Styro-type cups with the claim "CFCs Removed" are another poor choice because they support a throw-away mentality in consumers and end up taking years to biodegrade in our already stressed landfills. Plastic and Styrofoam products are often eaten by wildlife, especially birds. Some suggest that a paper cup would be a "friendlier" option, but the same "throw-away" thought process is involved. Any disposable item, whether "environmentally friendly" or not, is still waste. Environmentalists are calling this new type of consumer awareness the "cradle to grave" approach to buying. Using the case of the paper cup as an example, it works like this: A paper cup is made from a tree—possibly a several-hundred-year-old tree. A fossil fuel is burned to manufacture and package this bleached paper cup, which is then glued with vinyl acetate and colored with a cadium ink. More fossil fuels are burned to deliver this cup to market. You drive your car to the market to purchase the cup. You use it once, then dispose of it. It enters a landfill or is burned. Waste all the way around, and all so that you could have the "convenience" of disposing of a paper cup.

Consumers are bound to become cynical and defiant if manufacturers covertly continue to mislead them toward products that cause more harm than good. We must start to question the whole notion of "convenience" products.

learning activities

▶ Encourage your child to design a "green" label for environmentally conscious products. Send it to a consumer group for endorsement and promotion. Contact:

The Council on Economic Priorities
30 Irving Pl.
New York, NY 10003

How Can We Discern?

Co-op America is one nonprofit consumer group working to create a socially and environmentally responsible economy, and distributes a number of environmentally sound products and related information. It suggests a four-point economic strategy to help you make appropriate Earth-conscious decisions for your money.

▶ 1 Buy from environmentally sensitive businesses. Practice the "Three Rs" concept of Reduce, Reuse, and Recycle.

▶ **2** Invest in companies that contribute positively to the environment.

▶ **3** Boycott companies that continue to destroy the planet.

▶ **4** Demand change from businesses that are unwilling to adopt environmentally sound practices.

Another gauge for consumers is the use of the "green" description as outlined by the authors of *The Green Consumer,* John Elkington, Julia Hailes, and Joel Makower. "Green" is defined as:

▶ **1** Products with environmentally sound contents.

▶ **2** Products wrapped in environmentally sound packaging.

▶ **3** Both of the above.

The authors take "green" a step further with an ideological checklist for consumers to follow when shopping:

▶ **1** The product should not be dangerous to the health of humans or animals.

▶ **2** Green products do not cause damage to the planet during manufacture.

▶ **3** Green products do not consume disproportionate amounts of energy and other natural resources during their manufacture, use, or disposal.

▶ **4** Green products should not cause unnecessary waste due to excessive packaging or a short life.

▶ **5** These products are not associated with unnecessary use of or cruelty toward animals.

▶ **6** Green products do not use material derived from threatened species or limited natural resources.

learning activities
▶ **1** The chances are that everything you buy in the market has some effect on the environment. Determining what is least detrimental is the key to change. Discuss ways that this can be done. Discuss the alternatives to supermarkets in general, such as food cooperatives that generally sell many more green products, or buying directly from organic farms. Have the children investigate a few of these by starting in the telephone book. In the back of

environmentally oriented magazines there are often advertisements for mail order and other distributors of green products. Call to receive more information, and decide as a family if this is a choice you want to make.

▶ **2** When the moment seems right (you have energy, the kids are rested, there is no time constraint or pressure to buy, and you have money in the checkbook), attempt an environmentally focused shopping adventure. Keep the "less is best" philosophy in mind and ask yourself, What is the cradle-to-grave impact of this product on the planet? Is there an alternative product to replace the offending one and do you really need the product at all—is less best?

▶ **3** Shopping for a school friend's birthday present can be a prime time to attempt this event. Kids are excited to pick out a special gift and tend to stay in their "best behavior" mode in hopes of getting something for themselves, too. If you have more than one child, it may help to give your undivided attention to one child at a time. Shopping with one, making it a special parent-child adventure, and concluding with a special lunch or picnic may make the activity more memorable.

Begin with a discussion of what your needs are (budget limit, size) and talk about how it is important to choose something that won't hurt the planet and can be used for many years. If it is a birthday present, be creative and discuss alternatives to toys (bird feeders, books, clothing, gardening equipment, pets). Talk about the toys, too. Discuss how plastics hurt the planet when they are made and trashed. Suggest how easily they break. Examine the way products are packaged and suggest an unpackaged product (baseball bat, glove, ball, jump rope) to avoid throwaway material. How about the wrapping paper and card? You can buy recycled paper products or be creative at home using newspaper comics as the wrapping paper and creating an artistic, homemade card.

Use this as a starting point, a project that you can build on in future shopping trips. Before long, the kids will be leading you. It is so easy to teach this kind of environmentally conscious shopping behavior; the difficulty is in changing your past consumer habits. The challenge is to be consistent in setting your example.

SUPPORTING ENVIRONMENTALLY
SENSITIVE BUSINESSES

Keeping the above principles in mind, where can a consumer find such products? If you've been to your local supermarket or department store, you've noticed that the shelves are not exactly full of green products.

Buying products and services from environmentally sensitive businesses that work to protect the Earth is not as easy as it sounds. We must put our needs into perspective and set priorities for them by purchasing products which conserve rather than exploit the planet's natural resources. Keep in mind that green is also the color of money. Buying from green businesses can be frustrating because many of the price tags for their products are relatively high compared to more commercial products. One way to see beyond the numbers is to determine whether or not the company you are buying from contributes a portion of its proceeds to environmental organizations. Companies that "share the wealth" are generally environmentally sensitive and deserve your business.

You can also better understand the higher prices if you remember your high school economics and the law of supply and demand. The public is only just becoming aware of the availability of these products, and as demand increases, prices will become lower. Until then, it is worthwhile to shop and compare, just as you would for highly commercial goods.

Price-comparison shopping becomes easier once you are familiar with the market and have a variety of sources from which to draw. Mail-order catalogs are one way to do some shopping at home. By simply subscribing to a few "green" catalogs (and sharing them with your friends) you can familiarize yourself with the alternatives that are available, price-shop, and possibly contribute to environmental causes at the same time. The following are a few of the established, environmentally sensitive mail-order catalogs that will help you locate hard-to-find, planet-preserving merchandise such as solar appliances, recycled paper products, etc. Keep the cradle-to-grave concept in mind, and whenever possible order from the company located closest to you. The savings in energy used for extensive transport is yet another way to reduce air pollution.

Amway Corporation
Ada, MI 49355

Co-op America
10 Farrell St.
South Burlington, VT 05403

Ecco Bella
6 Provost Square, #602
Caldwell, NJ 07006

Eco-Choice
P.O. Box 281
Montvale, NJ 07645

Real Goods
966 Mazzoni St.
Ukiah, CA 95482

Seventh Generation
Colchester, VT 05446

Many of the larger environmental organizations have their own mail-order catalogs and sell merchandise to directly support their own causes. The following groups offer unique products that you may not find in other catalogs, or retail outlets:

Center for Marine Conservation
Catalog Department
P.O. Box 810
Old Saybrook, CT 06575

The Cousteau Society
930 W. 21st St.
Norfolk, VA 23517

Environmental Action
1525 New Hampshire Ave., N.W.
Washington, D.C. 20036

The Greenpeace Catalog
P.O. Box 77048
San Francisco, CA 94107

National Wildlife Federation
1400 16th St., N.W.
Washington, D.C. 20036

Sierra Club
P.O. Box 7959
San Francisco, CA 94120

REDUCE, REUSE, AND RECYCLE

To practice the philosophy of Reduce, Reuse, and Recycle in your shopping routine you and your child should consider:

▶ 1 Whether the product or package you choose to buy is something you can live without, even if it is advertised as an environmentally friendly product. Do the same as you flip through catalog pages and walk down supermarket aisles. This process will most likely eliminate products such as bleach, fabric softener, drain cleaners, air fresheners, disposable cameras, razors, pens, dishes, and utensils, electric can openers, and plastic trinkets.

▶ 2 Whether the product is manufactured in such a way that it is durable enough for reuse. Ideal choices include wooden toys which outlast plastics, cloth diapers which obviously outlast disposable, and replaceable razor blades which outlast the billions of disposable plastic models thrown away each year.

▶ 3 Your commitment to donating reusable items to charity or passing them on for others to use. This aspect is critical to the cycle. By discarding an old sofa or lawn chair with the weekly trash you are not helping the environment as much as you could if you donated it to charity or passed it along. Make an extra effort to call the local thrift shop to come and collect unwanted furniture. Return hangers to the dry cleaner. Reuse boxes, jars, bags, paper scraps, cards, envelopes, and rechargeable batteries.

Precycling

Precycling is a method of exercising your Earth-conscious ethics and taking this consciousness a step further before even buying a product. It is a means of making intelligent choices and actually reducing before you buy. If you practice the art of precycling, you will significantly reduce the amount of disposable waste that accumulates in your home—throw-away trash that fills our waste sites and pollutes our atmosphere and water supply. Here are a few tips to help you with this precycling effort:

▶ 1 Look for products in refillable or recyclable containers.

▶ 2 Buy in bulk or from bulk suppliers whenever possible.

▶ 3 Avoid disposable plastics, rigid foams, and excess packaging. Squeeze bottles, Styrofoam cartons, TV dinners with plastic dishes, and even items heat-sealed in plastic displays are all products available in less wasteful containers. According to The Earth Works Group in their book *50 Simple Things You Can Do to Save the Earth,* Americans spend one out of every eleven dollars used to buy food on packaging. If we consider all the consumer items we

buy each year, an outrageous amount of our income goes to the purchase of throw-away packaging.
▶ **4** Teach your children about excess packaging and show them examples of this in the grocery and their favorite toy store.
▶ **5** Start a precycling campaign in your community or school as a means of informing the public about the waste problem.

make a difference!

▶ **1** Rent or borrow products that you do not often use. If you use these products on a frequent basis, consider shopping for them at yard sales, through the want ads, or in thrift shops. For larger, more expensive items, such as a lawn mower, consider inviting several neighbors to purchase one that can be shared throughout the neighborhood. This could also work for carpet steam cleaners, floor polishers, heavy tools, etc.
▶ **2** Try to avoid the purchase of "convenience" products when there are suitable alternatives. Aerosols and sprays are considered conveniences. Search out alternatives to products such as spot removers, oven cleaners, fabric protectors, furniture polish, hair sprays, and air fresheners. Most of these come in some easy-to-apply cream or solid that is as effective as a spray or aerosol and much less harmful to the air.
▶ **3** Examine your decision to purchase paper plates, cups, napkins, paper towels, and plastic utensils. If you cannot always use a cloth or sponge to wipe up spills, or cloth napkins, or washable dinnerware, consider buying recycled paper products. The following companies offer recycled paper alternatives:

Ashdun Industries Inc.
16605 John St.
Fort Lee, NJ 07024

We Recycle Unlimited
P.O. Box 275-E
Cape Porpoise, ME 04104

Statler Tissue
300 Middlesex Ave.
Medford, MA 02155

Winter White
P.O. Box 40516
Grand Junction, CO 81504

▶ **4** Avoid plastic products. Wash eating utensils and dishes rather than purchasing plastic. Rent or borrow these supplies for parties and barbecues rather than buying throw-aways. If plastic is your only choice, reuse or recycle it.

▶ 5 Look for alternatives to cheap toys, kids' furniture, and plastic inflatable devices. These do not generally last long and repairs are not always successful or long-lasting. When shopping for toys and furniture for your child, consider some of the quality merchandise carried in the following catalogs:

Amish Country Collection
P.O. Box 5085
New Castle, PA 16105

Animal Town Game Company
P.O. Box 2002
Santa Barbara, CA 93120

Country Workshop
95 Rome St.
Newark, NJ 07105

Hartline
3 Crafts Rd.
Gloucester, MA 01930

Hearthsong
P.O. Box B
Sebastapol, CA 95473

Learning Materials Workshop
58 Henry St.
Burlington, VT 05401

Museum of the American
  Indian
Broadway at 155th St.
New York, NY 10032

Music for Little People
P.O. Box 1460
Redway, CA 95560

North Star Toys
617 North Star Route
Questa, NM 87556

Renew America
1400 16th St., N.W.
Washington, D.C. 20036

The Ridge Company
P.O. Box 2859
South Bend, IN 46680

Smithsonian Institution
Dept. 0006
Washington, D.C. 20073

Tryon Toymakers
1851 Redland Road
Campobello, SC 29322

Wisconsin Wagon Co.
507 Laurel Ave.
Janesville, WI 53545

Woodmonger
111 N. Siwash
Tonasket, WA 98855

▶ **6** Rather than buying it, make it. Hobbies are a great way to relieve stress, and offer excellent opportunities for family projects. Sewing or woodworking may be just the hobby for you. Those interested in sewing or needlework can contact their local fabric store or recreation department for the availability of instructional classes. Try some of the following woodworking catalogs to get started on building instead of buying toys and furniture. Any child would delight in sleeping in a bed he helped to make.

This company makes colonial furniture including a child-size chair and Windsor high chair. Kits are available.

Cohasset Colonials by Hagerly
Cohasset, MA 02025

The following offer blueprint patterns for making wooden toys, games, puzzles, and much more.

Design Group
P.O. Box 514
Miller Place, NY 11764

Toys and Joys
P.O. Box 628
Lynden, WA 98264

Julia Toys
1283 Avery Court
St. Louis, MO 63122

U-Build
P.O. Box 2383
Van Nuys, CA 91409

Toy Designs
P.O. Box 441
Newton, IA 50208

For the sewing enthusiast, this firm sells patterns for sewing traditional Amish clothing.

Friends
50305 S.R. 145
Woodsfield, OH 43793

▶ **7** Rather than throwing out old toys, make it a practice to do a yearly sweep and donate them to a worthy cause. Most charitable organizations will even provide a curbside pick-up service, especially during the holiday season.

- Consider organizing a neighborhood "toy library." A neighbor with a large attic or room in the basement can donate the space. Old toys, or toys no longer of interest to your child, can be put in the library. Children may "borrow" the toys for a designated period of time (a month is a reasonable length of time) and then return them for another "loan." This is an excellent way to reuse or recycle toys that would otherwise find themselves in the dumpster.

- For information about more formal toy-lending programs in your area, contact the:

Toy Library Association
2719 Broadway Ave.
Evanston, IL 60201

- Consider organizing a family or neighborhood yard sale, not just for toys, but for all the household goods you have no further interest in keeping. Think of creative, conscientious ways to spend the proceeds. Perhaps you could adopt an acre of rain forest from The Nature Conservancy, buy a subscription to *P-3*, an environmental magazine for children, or buy a few trees to plant in your yard. Any number of environmental contributions are possible.

▶ 8 Purchase clothing "built to last." The companies listed below make high-quality, long-lasting clothing for all ages. Some of these also support environmental organizations as corporate sponsors.

Patagonia Mail Order, Inc.
P.O. Box 8900
Bozeman, MT 59715

REI
P.O. Box 88125
Seattle, WA 981387

Piragis Northwoods
The Boundary Waters Catalog
105 N. Central Ave.
Ely, MN 55731

The catalogs listed below specialize in clothing for children.

After the Stork
1501 12th St., N.W.
Albuquerque, NM 87104

Hanna Andersson
1010 N.W. Flanders
Portland, OR 97209

Biobottoms
P.O. Box 6009
Petaluma, CA 94953

▶ **9** Avoid purchasing products that are made from animals or tropical woods.

▶ **10** Instead of buying a second car, consider purchasing a new bike and a bike trailer to carry the groceries and the kids. Ride instead of drive.

▶ **11** When shopping for gifts consider nature and science products. The following businesses give a percentage of their profits back to environmental causes.

Audubon Workshop
1501 Paddock Dr.
Northbrook, IL 60062

Center for Environmental Education
P.O. Box 810
Old Saybrook, CT 06475

The Nature Company
P.O. Box 2310
Berkeley, CA 94702

(The Nature Company also has a number of retail outlets around the country. Consult your telephone book for a store in your area.)

▶ **12** Buy milk and juice in reusable or recyclable glass. Choose plastic or juice cans as the next best option, and recycle the containers. Avoid cartons and aseptic boxes that create bulk trash.

▶ **13** Avoid disposable diapers; use cloth or a diaper service.

The Natural Baby Co.
Rt. 1, Box 160
Titusville, NJ 08560

•

ENVIRONMENTALLY RESPONSIBLE PRODUCTS

The Vermont Country Store
Mail Order Office
P.O. Box 3000
Manchester Center, VT 05255

▶ **14** Do you read all of those daily newspapers? If the answer is no, discontinue the daily and buy the weekend edition. Choose only one newspaper delivery rather than two. One weekly newspaper subscription will meet most needs.

▶ **15** Reuse your mail-order boxes to ship personal birthday and holiday packages.

- Use real popcorn as "loose fill" to pad the contents. It has been tested and is an excellent alternative to the Styrofoam peanuts or newspaper commonly used. It should not be eaten, however. Either save it for another package, or bring it along on your next nature walk to feed the birds.
- Reuse envelopes and padded mailers.

▶ **16** Buying a battery recharger will reduce toxic waste. Reusable nickel-cadmium batteries are a worthwhile investment. They may be a more expensive option, but the savings are tremendous, especially when you have small children who go through batteries quickly. For a reliable model contact:

Sunwatt Corporation
RFD Box 751
Addison, ME 04606

▶ **17** Consider alternatives to toxic beauty supplies. Some common toxins include hair dyes, nail polish, nail polish removers, perfumes, talc powders, and permanent-wave preparations. There are now "green" cosmetics which use fewer natural resources, require less energy to produce, have minimal packaging, are not tested on animals, and contain no animal by-products. Cruelty issues aside, animal-derived cosmetic ingredients are often slaughterhouse by-products.

Manufacturers often have a choice in how they will obtain their ingredients. For example, "green" companies seeking purity in the products make their glycerins from nonoffensive coconut oil rather than residue beef tallow.

Excess packaging is yet another offense of many cosmetic companies. "Green" manufacturers who use plastic choose recyclable containers that use a voluntary coding system to help facilitate post-consumption recycling. Patronize the following green companies:

Aubrey Organics
4419 North Manhattan Ave.
Tampa, FL 33614

Beauty Without Cruelty
Pamela Marsen, Inc.
P.O. Box 119
Teaneck, NJ 07666

Autumn Harp
28 Rockydale Rd.
Bristol, VT 05443

The Body Shop
45 Horsehill Rd.
Cedar Knolls, NJ 07927

▶ **18** If yours is a family that gardens, here are two mail-order garden suppliers that carry kid-sized tools:

Henry Field Seed & Nursery Co.
Shenandoah, IA 51602

Plow & Hearth
560 Main St.
Madison, VA 22727

The following is a list of organic garden suppliers:

Gardener's Supply
128 Intervale Rd.
Burlington, VT 05401

Natural Gardening Research
  Center
P.O. Box 149
Sunman, IN 47041

Growing Naturally
P.O. Box 54
Pineville, PA 18946

Peaceful Valley Farm Supply
P.O. Box 2209
Grass Valley, CA 95945

Integrated Fertility Management
333 Ohme Gardens Rd.
Wenatchee, WA 98801

▶ **19** Buy reusable lunch bags, boxes, food containers, and cellulose sandwich bags instead of plastic ones. Cellulose food storage bags are made from wood pulp and can degrade much faster than plastic. When you are finished with them, they can be tossed in the compost pile for recycling.

Earth Care Paper, Inc.
P.O. Box 3335
Madison, WI 53704

Better still, use plastic containers that can be reused over and over again for school and office lunches.

▶ **20** Consider planet-saving products for your home. The following companies concentrate their efforts on providing environmentally safe household goods. Focus is placed on nontoxic, nonpolluting, resource-saving products that are both efficient and convenient. If these manufacturers have retailers near you, they will refer you to the appropriate store in your area. However, many of these products are only shipped directly from the manufacturer.

AIR-SAVING PRODUCTS
Air-cleaning systems:

Atlantic Environmental Products Corporation
Hepacare Air System
725 Church St., 17th Fl.
Lynchburg, VA 24504

Berner Air Products, Inc.
P.O. Box 5410
New Castle, PA 16105

Energy-efficient lights, fixtures, and products:

A Brighter Way
P.O. Box 18446
Austin, TX 78760

The Energy Store
P.O. Box 3507
Santa Cruz, CA 95063

Environmentally responsible paints, solvents, and cleaning products:

BAU, Inc.
7 Hills Ave.
Concord, NH 03301

Eco Design Co.
1365 Rufina Cr.
Santa Fe, NM 87501

Sinan Co.
Natural Building Materials
Auro Organic Paint
P.O. Box 181
Suisun City, CA 94585

Mail-order solar products and propane appliances:

American Solar Network, Ltd.
12811 Bexhill Ct.
Herndon, VA 22071

Energy Federation, Inc.
354 Waverly St.
Framingham, MA 01701

Suntools
271 Franklin Ave.
Willitis, CA 95490
(Solar car kit)

LAND-NURTURING PRODUCTS
Paper supplies:

Acorn Designs
5066 Mott Evan Rd.
Trumansburg, NY 14886

Alte Schule USA
1365 Rufina Cr.
Santa Fe, NM 87501

Conservatree
10 Lombard St., Suite 250
San Francisco, CA 94111

PRODUCTS FOR THE CHEMICALLY SENSITIVE

Healthy House Catalog
Environmental Health Watch
4115 Bridge Ave.
Cleveland, OH 44113

WATER-SAVING PRODUCTS
Toilet dams, low-flow faucet aerators, and low-flow toilets:

Seventh Generation
Colchester, VT 05446-1672

▶ **21** Make efforts to avoid bleach and bleached products. Most white-paper products, including toilet paper and women's personal hygiene products, use bleached paper which contains dioxins, a highly toxic group of environmental pollutants. Dioxins are formed during paper production as a result of using chlorine compounds to bleach the pulp to make the paper white. These contaminants, since they are present in numerous personal-care products made of paper, then come in contact with the skin. Paper towels, facial tissue, toilet paper, disposable diapers, and feminine-hygiene products are all examples. The same contaminants have also been found in paper packaging that comes in contact with foods and beverages.

A wide selection of unbleached paper and cotton products can be found in the Seventh Generation catalog listed above.

Alternative unbleached feminine-hygiene products:

The Keeper
Box 20023
Cincinnati, OH 45220

Sea Sponge
P.O. Box 680
South Sutton, NH 03273

Mood Pads
P.O. Box 166
Boulder Creek, CA 95006

▶ **22** Avoid purchasing single-serving-size snack packages. Consider purchasing snack items in bulk and providing a reusable container which can be filled as needed.

As a society of consumers, we have been raised to take "convenience" for granted. Technology has blurred our vision and common sense. Congratulate yourself and your child for every small change that you are willing to make. This Earth-conscious buying is not easy. It is a lifelong learning process.

learning activities

▶ 1 As an experiment, save and sort all of the packaging you normally throw away in a week. This is an excellent activity for children to do on their own. Doing so will give you an excellent—and perhaps appalling—idea of how much waste is actually generated by the items you purchase. Include all cardboard boxes, cans, bottles, jars, plastic bags, plastic bottles, anything that contains a product. We guarantee that the minimountain you create will be an eye-opener.

Make an effort to locate a recycling center in your area. Most smaller recycling operations restrict the items that they accept for recycling; they will take paper and glass, but you may need to do some research to find one that will accept cardboard, plastic, tin, and aluminum.

▶ 2 The next time the children start asking for a heavily advertised toy (Barbie, board games, water games, or GI Joe, for example), suggest a tour of local thrift shops. You can usually find a treasure or two to suit your child's fancy. When you shop at thrift shops or yard sales, you can count on a good price and are practicing and teaching the concept of reuse.

▶ 3 Buy some fabric paint and bandannas or linen napkins and have the kids decorate their own napkins. These cloth alternatives will eliminate the need for paper napkins at the dinner table and will wash easily for years to come.

ECO INVESTMENTS

For those of you who have more disposable income, there are additional routes you can take in your effort to support socially and environmentally responsible businesses.

Economists suggest that not only should we buy green products, but we can help even more by directly supporting companies that contribute positively to the environment. This can be done by investing our money in companies which:

▶ 1 Produce green products;

▶ 2 Engage in the research and development of new, clean technologies such as alternative energy;

▶ 3 Participate in industrial cleanup activities, such as manufacturing pollution-control apparatus and operating recycling plants.

For more information about socially responsible investing, contact the:

Social Investment Forum
430 First Ave. North
Minneapolis, MN 55401

The following socially responsible companies can help you to choose worthwhile investments. If you're thinking about saving for your children's education, choosing socially responsible investments will give that process a brighter edge.money, their profits drop—something no CEO wants to see happen.

New Alternatives Fund
295 Northern Blvd.
Great Neck, NY 11021
516-466-0808

Pax World Fund
224 State St.
Portsmouth, NH 03801
603-431-8022

Socially Responsible Banking
  Fund
Vermont National Bank
P.O. Box 804
Brattleboro, VT 05301
800-544-7108

The Social Responsibility
  Investment Group
127 Peachtree St., N.E.
Atlanta, GA 30303
404-577-3635

Working Assets Money Fund
230 California St.
San Francisco, CA 94111
800-533-FUND (3963)

BOYCOTTS

Talking to children about boycotts will help them make sense of all the changes you make. Discussing why you no longer buy a particular product will help the family understand the absence of some of their favorite treats.

By avoiding and actively rejecting the purchase of certain products from environmental offenders, we send a powerful message to the management of these companies. When we withhold our money, their profits drop—something no CEO wants to see happen. The advantage of a boycott is that it is legal: Anyone can be involved and it hits companies where it counts, in their profit and loss columns. Historically, refusal to buy products has been an effective message to manufacturers. The more visible and talked about the boycott is, the more successful the results will be.

As recently as 1990, a boycott against tuna fish resulted in massive changes within the United States. When profits fell drastically, American companies felt compelled to alter their method of catching tuna or reconsider from whom they would purchase it. You'll recall the tragedy of hundreds of dolphins and other marine life being killed in the nets commonly used to catch tuna. The switch has been made (for the most part) to "dolphin safe" tuna.

It took years of campaigning by Greenpeace volunteers and consumers before this issue received the visibility it needed to influence change. But the message is clear, *boycotts do work.* Collective consumer voices cause a mighty roar in the ear of irresponsible corporations, forcing them to take action.

The trick to successful boycotts is knowing who the offenders are and what products they manufacture. Did you know that popular "acid washed" jeans are an eco-oversight simply because we are not aware of abusive manufacturers? The pumice that softens and fades this popular fashion item is strip-mined, a process which involves destroying forests and threatening water tables; it results in the removal of precious topsoil that leaves the forest unjustifiably scarred.

Most violating companies keep a tight lid on their environmental abuse. However, there is a resource available to help you. *Shopping for a Better World,* produced by The Council on Economic Priorities, offers consumers a quick and easy guide to the practices of the companies that manufacture your favorite products. This easy-to-read book (which fits easily in a pocket so that you can carry it with you on your shopping excursions) measures the social responsibility of hundreds of companies by rating them in eleven different categories:

•

ENVIRONMENTALLY RESPONSIBLE PRODUCTS

▶ **1** Charitable contributions
▶ **2** Women's advancement
▶ **3** Minority advancement
▶ **4** Military contracts
▶ **5** Animal testing
▶ **6** Disclosure of information
▶ **7** Community outreach
▶ **8** Nuclear power
▶ **9** Involvement in South Africa
▶ **10** Commitment to the environment
▶ **11** Family benefits

By simply looking up your favorite food or consumer item you will see a rating for each of the eleven categories. The graphic symbols will help you decide whether or not you want to continue to patronize a company or seek a satisfactory alternative. (See Chapter 9 for further information on obtaining a copy of this book.)

Sources of information regarding specific boycotts can be found in:

Action Boycott News
Co-op America
2100 M St., N.W., Suite 310
Washington, D.C. 20063

The National Boycott News
Institute for Consumer Responsibility
6506 28th Ave., N.E.
Seattle, WA 98115

A combination of letter writing and an active, consistent boycott of products is an intelligent method for seeking change. Regardless of the results, you will feel good about your efforts to influence change and teach your child the value of working for change.

the valdez principles

Buying green and investing in green companies contributes to the support of a planet-saving economy. Active boycotts and letter writing (we'll give you some tips on letter writing in Appendix 3) balance the process by demanding changes from the offenders. To take this process a step further, Co-op America is leading a campaign that encourages companies to sign the "Valdez Principles." This concept includes ten clear-cut guidelines that arose out of the disastrous *Valdez* oil spill in Alaska in 1989. The Valdez Principles define what businesses must do to protect the environment.

1 PROTECTION OF THE BIOSPHERE. Companies must make an effort to reduce the amount of pollutants that are released into our water, air, and earth.

2 SUSTAINABLE USE OF NATURAL RESOURCES. Companies will engage in the sustainable use of renewable natural resources.

3 REDUCTION OF DISPOSABLE WASTE. Companies will work to reduce hazardous waste, and recycle whenever possible. Waste will be handled safely and responsibly.

4 WISE USE OF ENERGY. Companies will make an effort to use sustainable and renewable energy sources.

5 RISK REDUCTION. Companies will work to ensure that their practices are safe for employees, communities, and the environment, and will be prepared in the event of an emergency.

6 MARKETING OF SAFE PRODUCTS AND SERVICES. Companies will sell products that interfere as little as possible with the Earth's natural processes, and are safe for consumer use.

7 DAMAGE COMPENSATION. Companies will assume responsibility for any damage inflicted on the environment through cleanup and compensation.

8 DISCLOSURE. Companies will inform communities of any environmental damage caused by their practices.

9 ENVIRONMENTAL DIRECTORS AND MANAGERS. At least one member of the board of directors would be qualified to represent environmental interests.

10 ASSESSMENT AND ANNUAL AUDIT. Companies will conduct
a yearly assessment of their adoption of these principles, and
inform the public of the results.

Your support of these principles by your support of the companies which are working to adopt them is a valuable contribution to
the encouragement of manufacturer responsibility and the development of green products for you and your child. It will not happen
if you do not let the corporate world know what you expect from the
products you buy, and that you will actively boycott products that
are clear violations of environmental responsibility.

learning activity

▶ Buy or borrow a copy of *Shopping for a Better World* (see
Chapter 9 for details). Spend a few moments with your child, looking up your most frequent food purchases. How do the companies
that produce them fare according to the rating system? Are there
alternative products/companies that you could choose?

the politics of food

This bread I bake was once the oat . . .

Dylan Thomas

IT is food which propels the human machine and gives us the energy to work, play, think, and create. Without it we would not grow, keep warm, or get better if we became ill. We need a variety of healthy foods to keep us going. Our ideas on just what those healthy foods are has changed somewhat over the years.

In recent years it has become generally accepted by concerned individuals that "eating lower on the food chain"—or decreasing the amount of meat and animal by-products we consume, and increasing our intake of fresh fruits and vegetables—is a sound way to create a healthier body for ourselves and our children. Just as important, it provides a responsible course for our use of the environment.

Everywhere we look, we see our culture demanding slim, healthy bodies and urging us to eat well and exercise regularly. Television and magazine advertisements now promote "lite" products, the importance of fiber in all its forms, the promise of bran, low-salt reduced-calorie goodies, all followed by inspiring solicitations for health clubs.

But have you ever noticed the ads aimed at our children? Fast-food, high-fat, Styrofoam-encased burgers, sugar-laden cereals, empty-calorie candy bars . . . We encourage and accept our children's consumption of bad food during childhood but then insist in early adulthood that they adopt completely opposite eating habits and start consuming good food. The lack of sense in that turnaround escapes all of us.

issue

We're infinitely attracted to the convenient, attractive package regardless of what's inside. We are more concerned with the ease of shopping for and preparing a food item, and how quick it is to eat, than we are in what that item wastes in nutrition, calories, and packaging. Our overburdened landfills are overflowing with plastic microwave dinner plates, and our stomachs with salty, processed, chemically preserved, and frozen foods.

We need to be concerned about food production from seed to store—how our food is grown, harvested, marketed, and arrives on our tables—and know, too, that alternatives to traditional practice are gaining in prominence.

If we, as adults who've read all the statistics and paid attention to the advice of countless nutritionists, can focus on sensible eating habits, we have only to gain: in good health for ourselves, and choices that will benefit our growing children into their own adulthood.

Somewhere the parent of a ten-year-old is reading this, shaking her head, moaning, and feeling at a loss as her child dips a hungry hand into a plastic bag full of something crunchy (and it probably isn't Brazil nuts). This chapter will do its best to help all of you who face a similar dilemma. Eating certain foods is a habit. It was made. It can be broken. With a few tricks and a little valuable information, we'll help you to understand the necessity for responsible eating, not just for dietary reasons, but for the social implications as well; and how to ease your kids into this unknown territory with an educated, gentle hand. By the end of this chapter you should have a confident handle on why food choices are not only a personal concern, but why they have a direct effect on our environment and economy as well. What's more, you'll be doing your child a tremendous service by setting a pattern of healthy, responsible eating.

Much of what we suggest will require that you set aside many of your traditional concepts about food and be open to the introduction of new information. No, we're not trying to turn you into a vegetarian. But there are some interesting points to be made about the way we eat, and what we eat.

EATING LOWER
ON THE FOOD CHAIN

The phrase itself has always been popular among vegetarians and other nutritionally conscious people, but it is gaining in popularity now that eating habits are being discussed in more classrooms and kitchens around the country. In these discussions, themes other than nutrition are beginning to emerge. We've begun to consider, for example, the effect that cattle/livestock ranching has on our own natural resources, and those of other countries—the rain forests of Central America, for example.

From a nutritional viewpoint, it is estimated that Americans consume almost twice the amount of protein that the body needs. Since protein cannot be stored in the body, it is either burned in place of carbohydrates or eliminated as waste. And yet the "meat" portion of a meal continues to define the nature of that meal. When your child asks, "What's for dinner" how often do you answer, "Lamb chops," or "Steak," or "Roast," or "Beef stew," and never name the vegetables that may be accompanying it? These answers are the same ones parents have been giving their children for years.

Our dependence on this protein myth has completely shaped our notion of "meal." We've long believed that meat is the best source of protein, the food highest in protein content and quality. In fact, meat falls somewhere in the middle of the protein scale, and eggs, fish, milk, cheese, and soybeans rank higher. We've believed that meat protein is the best source when, in reality, a greater percentage of the protein found in eggs and milk is absorbed by the body. Conversely, we've accepted the misconception that plant protein is an inferior protein. Though it does lack certain essential amino acids, if vegetable protein is eaten in combination with other foods it can provide equal or better protein. Finally, even if we're aware of all this rather technical information about food, we believe that vegetable-oriented diets are boring. No doubt this is true if you consider our dependence on a rather limited selection of mostly domestic crops. There are dozens of edible plants waiting to be cultivated and introduced into the American diet—many from the tropical forests of Latin America, for example—but we remain enamored of those that slide out of a can or a frozen plastic bag. If we continue to live and eat this way, there is little doubt that we will pass the same attitude toward food down to the children we feed every day. We'll discuss changing this behavior later in the chapter. What follows are the related issues that define the "food" discussion.

Animal Agriculture and Natural Resources

According to *Diet for a New America*, by John Robbins, if Americans were to lower their meat consumption by as little as 10 percent, the amount of grain and soybeans saved would feed the 60 million people who annually die of starvation around the world. Startling? Yes. Here's more:

- Sixteen pounds of grain and 2,500 gallons of water are needed to produce one pound of beef.
- Livestock production consumes more than half of all the water used in the United States.
- One-third of the North American land surface is devoted to cattle grazing.
- In an ironic twist, cattle may actually be contributing to the greenhouse effect. Methane, a powerful gas which is responsible for about 20 percent of the greenhouse effect, comes from cattle flatulence.

- Two hundred and twenty million acres of forest in America; an area the size of Austria in Brazil; and half of all Central American rain forests have been cut for livestock production.
- Growing fruits, vegetables, and grains uses less than 5 percent of the raw materials needed for meat production.

make a difference!

▶ 1 The greatest contribution you can make, even if you are a committed meat eater, is to cut down on the quantity you eat. Think about what even a 10 percent reduction will save.

▶ 2 How about planting a garden? It's America's favorite recreational activity. Why not make it one of yours? You can plant any number of edible goodies in any size plot of land—even in pots. Assign your children their own section of the garden, or give them a few pots and let them grow their own herbs and vegetables.

learning activities

▶ 1 Give vegetables a chance! There are any number of excellent vegetable-oriented cookbooks on the market today. *The Moosewood Cookbook* and *The Enchanted Broccoli Forest,* both by M. Katzen, are among the many titles available. Talk to your local librarian or bookseller for the newest offerings. Better still, have your child do it. Make it a weekend project to go to the library and choose a cookbook. Ask if there are any specifically written for children.

▶ 2 Support your local "farmers market." In many communities across the country, local small-scale farmers gather—usually on weekends—to sell their produce. These farmers tend to be more environmentally conscious than larger-scale farmers. The prices are good, and the produce much fresher. It's a great Saturday morning family activity and a good opportunity for children to talk to farmers firsthand. You can even help them prepare a list of questions that are certain to receive willing answers. Some examples:

- "How long does it take an apple (green pepper, potato, etc.) to grow?"
- "How do you know when it is ready to be picked?"
- "How many grow on a tree (bush, vine, etc.)?"

- "Who picks the fruit (vegetables)?"
- "Do you sell any to the grocery stores?"

Be creative. Let your child be creative. Bring along a camera and record the experience—maybe even put together a little story when you're done.

Rain Forest vs. Animal Agriculture

As we've already discussed, the planet is losing trees—indeed, whole forests—at an alarming rate. With their destruction comes the loss of untold species of plants and animals that could be important sources of food for all of us. Nowhere is the devastation felt more intensely than in the tropical rain forests of South and Central America. It is estimated that these forests are disappearing at the rate of 27 million acres per year, or 67 acres per minute. The decimation process, called "slash and burn," was designed to eradicate as much vegetation as possible with the least amount of effort, and to create cattle-grazing land in its place. Only about 2 percent of the beef raised on this land is used in the United States, generally in fast-food restaurants. While this seems like a relatively low percentage, The Rainforest Action Network (RAN), a San Francisco–based organization, tells us that the production of a four-ounce hamburger patty represents the destruction of about 55 square feet of tropical rain forest, affecting thousands of species of plants, animals, insects, and birds. Multiply this by the millions of fast-food burgers consumed daily, and the number of destroyed trees and animals will frighten you.

Not much of this beef appears in your local supermarkets. It has a tendency to be tough and stringy, suitable only for combination with fattier meats and cereal fillers (as is the practice in fast-food restaurants). If you are concerned about your favorite fast-food restaurant's use of rain forest beef, contact one of the rain forest protection organizations mentioned earlier in the book. They will be able to provide you with the most current list of companies using rain forest beef.

Fast-food hamburgers aren't the only culprits in this crime against the rain forests. RAN also suggests that you avoid processed beef products such as baby foods, lunch meats, canned beef products, soups, and pet foods.

A further concern about this beef is its tendency to contain higher levels of toxic chemicals (pesticides) and trace metals. If those are present in the beef you eat, they will transfer to your body.

Foods from the Rain Forest

Numerous research projects are being undertaken by the scientific community to determine the extent to which species variety plays a role in the eating habits of Central American people. An example of this: There are well over fifty varieties of potatoes eaten in Latin America, while here in the United States, where massive quantities of the vegetable are consumed, we are dependent on just three or four varieties. In the produce sections of many Latin American supermarkets the variety of potato species occupies one and sometimes two entire aisles! Why haven't we attempted to cultivate these others? Habit. Wouldn't the economic possibilities be tremendous for our own farmers as well as those in Latin America if we did? This is true for many foods produced in Latin America, especially rain forest products. What better way to protect these precious ecological areas than to promote the responsible farming and harvesting of food products from sustainably managed forests?

The most common imported rain forest edibles currently found on supermarket shelves are nuts—especially Brazil nuts and cashews. In fact, Brazil nuts can be grown only in rain forests. Attempts at plantation cultivation have unfortunately met with failure. The nuts provide an excellent economic incentive for cultivating rather than destroying the rain forest. The same is true of cashews. Not only does the harvesting of cashew nuts promote rain forest protection, it is actually five times as profitable as cattle ranching, the most common reason for the destruction in the first place.

If you have trouble finding these products on your grocery store shelves, there are several organizations that sell them by mail order, with a large percentage of their profits going to organizations working to protect rain forests. In any case, exercise your consumer voice by asking your store managers to provide and promote these products.

make a difference!

▶ **1** Avoid buying beef produced in the rain forest. Identification can be difficult, but find the time to contact an organization specializing in rain forest issues and get their recommendations.

▶ **2** Support sustainably managed rain forest products: foods and other products harvested from the rain forest without harming or disturbing the life within it—Brazil nuts, cashews, bananas, coffee, cinnamon, chocolate, etc.

▶ **3** Teach your children about the wonders of the rain forest—foster respect. Help them organize a Rain Forest Awareness Week at school or at home. Information on doing this is available from:

Creating Our Future
398 N. Ferndale
Mill Valley, CA 94941
415-381-6744

▶ **4** Support the organizations working to encourage safe harvesting of rain forest products.

▶ **5** Serve rain forest nuts at parties and pack them in school lunches. Talk to your child about why buying and eating these nuts is a good practice. They're highly nutritious and taste wonderful. Kids won't need much coaxing.

▶ **6** For a change of pace, consider cashew butter instead of the traditional peanut butter sandwich. Again, this is not always easy to find in supermarkets but most specialty (gourmet) shops do carry it. Better yet, make your own! To do so, follow the directions for making your own peanut butter at the end of this chapter.

▶ **7** Give Rainforest Crunch candy (a nut brittle made with nuts from Brazilian rain forests, attractively packaged in reusable tins or cardboard boxes) as gifts for teachers, co-workers, Mother's Day, or whenever the occasion for sweets arises.

▶ **8** Buy nuts in bulk from the organizations listed below.

▶ **9** Encourage your local grocery stores to carry rain forest edibles. Ask for the camu-camu fruit from Peru, or the cupuacu, or assai, or any number of other exotic marvels. They are almost always available at specialty grocery stores. Check the telephone book for one in your area.

▶ **10** Put these exotics in your child's lunch and let her share and pass along the rain forest treat.

Rain forest nuts are available from:

Cultural Survival Imports
11 Divinity Ave.
Cambridge, MA 02138
617-495-2562

Rainforest Crunch candy is available from:

Community Products
RD #2, Box 1950
Montpelier, VT 05602
802-229-1840

ORGANIC FOODS

There is little agreement as to the meaning of the terms "healthy," "natural," and "organic" (a word which encompasses the other two), but vendors frequently proclaim that such foods are safer and more nutritious than conventionally grown foods. Are they? Are these foods, promoted as the best means to achieve a lower-on-the-food-chain diet, truly the best choices? You'll need to decide.

The term "organic" has generally come to refer to foods grown without the use of pesticides to keep destructive insects at bay. It is this lack of toxic substances that gives organically grown foods an advantage over commercial products. Logically, what's less risky for humans to consume is also a safer choice for the environment, and thus deserves our support.

When you buy organic foods, you are often buying from "green" farmers committed to the sustainability of the environment. If we as consumers increase our use of organic foods, the law of supply and demand will send a strong message to commercial farmers and politicians about increased public awareness and concern about pesticide use and abuse of our food supply.

Organic Certification

Though regulated by the Food and Drug Administration (FDA), the United Fresh Fruit and Vegetable Association has come to agree upon a definition of what "organic" means. Foods that meet the following criteria are credited with being organic and are certified as such.

- Organic food production involves farm management practices that replenish and maintain soil fertility.
- Organic food will be determined as such by an independent third party certification program based on a nationally approved list of materials and practices.
- Organic food is documented and verified as such by comprehensive records of the production and handling systems.
- Only nationally approved materials can be used on the crops and land for a three-year period prior to harvest.
- The harvesting, preservation, storing, transportation, and marketing will all be done in accordance with a nationally approved list of materials and practices.
- Organic foods will meet all state and federal regulations governing the quality and safety of the food supply.

Also, to make sure something is truly organic, a number of states have enacted labeling laws. For further information about these labeling laws and reliable vendors, contact:

The Organic Foods Production Association
P.O. Box 31
Belchertown, MA 01007
413-323-6821

Food Cooperatives

Fraud and deception in the marketing of produce is always a possibility where the "organic" issue is involved. Storekeepers must depend on the honesty of distributors and they, in turn, must rely on the word of their suppliers. Because of this and the premium prices placed on "health" foods, it's not surprising that conventional foods are often substituted for organic foods, or that labels on food products are altered. One way of ensuring the integrity of the organic food you buy is to shop in food cooperatives.

A food cooperative is a business like any other. But it differs in one significant way—the business belongs to the people who use it. As a member of a cooperative, you share control of that co-op with the other members, equally. All decisions affecting the business must be decided upon by the membership. Members also volunteer their time working in the store.

Most food cooperatives in this country are committed to selling organic foods and work diligently to ensure that the best of these are provided to their membership. The benefits of co-op membership are substantial, the shortcomings few. The trick for you, the consumer, is to overcome the lure of successfully advertised and popular processed foods. These you will not find in a co-op. There may be some "supermarket withdrawal" to contend with, but the benefits will quickly make themselves felt. For more information about food cooperatives, contact:

Co-op America
2100 M St., N.W., Suite 310
Washington, D.C. 20036
202-872-5307

ORGANIC GARDENING

If the idea of growing your own organic foods is feasible from a space aspect, and appealing from a nutritional one, why not go ahead and fulfill your desire for fresh, safe produce?

Planting a garden is beneficial to both you and the environment. Trees are not the only forms of vegetation that absorb carbon dioxide. Your garden, whether it consists of vegetables, shrubs, or flowers, will do the same. In addition, organically grown vegetables require no chemicals and no energy-consuming transportation to reach a market. But by far the best reason for growing your own organic produce is the wonderfully fresh flavors these fruits and vegetables possess. They taste the way fruit and vegetables were meant to taste.

Think of your garden as its own contained ecosystem—one which you create. You'll notice as time passes the increased variety of birds, insects, and animal life that are attracted to your backyard habitat.

Growing your own food can do much for your mental, emotional, and physical well-being. It is both relaxing and satisfying to surround yourself with the earth and grow food for your family. People have been engaged in this most basic of activities for centuries. But why should you engage in it now, during this age of convenience shopping?

- A healthy garden provides you and your child with a healthier and more diverse diet. How many times have you opted not to buy a particular fruit or vegetable at the market because it was too expensive, too stale, or too puny for the price?
- A healthy garden provides healthy food which in turn contributes to a sound mind and body.
- Growing your own keeps you from being affected by fluctuations in price which often depend on the weather.
- An organic garden helps to keep the soil, air, and groundwater pure.
- Growing a garden gives you the satisfaction of self-sufficiency as you watch "nothing" blossom into a plot of delicious produce.

Here are a few tips to help you get your garden started.

▶ **1** If you are a novice gardener, start with a small plot, a limited number of plants, and crops that are relatively easy to grow. Vegetables like carrots, potatoes, beans, lettuce, and tomatoes are all good choices. Starter plants are available for immediate planting in your garden, or you can start them yourself from seed.

▶ **2** If you have enough interested neighbors and an adequate plot of land to satisfy everyone's needs, consider creating a "community garden." Community gardens have been springing up all over the country. As well as being excellent sources of healthy food, they are a wonderful way for neighbors of all ages to spend time with one another, sharing food, recipes, and community spirit.

• For information on how to start a community garden, order a "Community Gardens Organizer's Kit" by contacting the:

National Gardening Association
180 Flynn Ave.
Burlington, VT 05401

▶ **3** Avoiding the use of chemicals can be difficult when growing a garden, but there are resources available to help you. If you can't find the following books in a local bookstore, consult your local library.

The Encyclopedia of Natural Insect and Disease Control: The Most Comprehensive Guide to Protecting Plants—Vegetables, Fruit, Flowers, Trees, and Lawns, Roger B. Yepsen, Editor. Rodale Press, Inc., 1984.

Good Neighbors: Companion Planting for Gardeners by Anna Carr. Rodale Press, Inc., 1985.

▶ **4** To make an all-purpose pest control spray, combine the following ingredients:

one garlic bulb
one small onion
one tablespoon of cayenne pepper
one tablespoon of liquid soap (as mild as possible)
one quart of water

Grind the garlic and onion and mix well with the water and the pepper.

Let the solution sit for one hour. It can be stored in a well-sealed jar in the refrigerator for up to one week.

Strain the mixture and put it in a spray bottle. Apply the spray as needed.

▶ **5** A tried-and-true method of garden pest control is to plant French marigolds in and around the produce beds. Many pests steer clear of these flowers. Ask your nursery for French marigold seeds or order them from:

Peaceful Valley Farm Supply
11173 Peaceful Valley Rd.
Nevada City, CA 95959

PACKAGING

We love packaging, and the advertising agencies whose job it is to sell us products know we love it. Nearly every food product we buy is wrapped in something. Even when the fresh fruits and vegetables found in the produce section are not packaged, we feel obligated to put them in plastic bags before weighing them. It is estimated that 30 percent of our overflowing landfills consists of packaging, roughly 1,800 pounds of it for every man, woman, and child each year.

Advertisers burn the midnight oil to design packaging that will grab our attention away from other products, and weave their packaging ploys into clever television ads that make us want whatever is being sold, regardless of the impact on our health or environment. Have you noticed the recent surge in "convenience" packaging, all designed so that you don't even have to dirty a dish to eat the contents? Unfortunately, most of these are plastic- or Styrofoam-based, and hence require recycling.

Packaging can be deceptive in one other significant way— language. There is a growing collection of packaging words— "natural," "organic," "biodegradable"—meant to entice us into the belief that the contents are safe. They are not always accurately used, especially by manufacturing conglomerates solely interested in making a sale. Read the content labels very carefully and apply the knowledge you've learned so far to make educated choices.

make a difference!

▶ **1** Work diligently to decrease the amount of television you and your child watch. Powerful subliminal messages that create unnecessary wants in your child will leave all of you frustrated.

▶ **2** Take advantage of having your kids along at the market by teaching them to be smart shoppers. Discussing why you make the choices you do and involving them in the buying process can help cut down on the inevitable "Can I have this?" and "Can I have that?"

- Talk to them about the importance of reading labels, and show them what you are looking for and why.
- Discuss the negative aspects of overpackaging by showing them examples. There are hundreds of overpackaged products on the shelves.
- Show them the difference between a recyclable container and a nonrecyclable one. Glass is the best example of a recyclable container, and heavy plastic ones, such as toothpaste pump dispensers, are among the worst.
- Point out the difference between fresh produce and that which has been sitting out too long.
- Teach them about shopping the perimeters of the grocery store. Most of the healthy, unpackaged food is at either end of the store. All packaged foods are found in the center aisles.

▶ **3** Choose products that do not come in fancy, nonrecyclable packaging. After all, its cost is added to that of the item, and you are paying for it. The Earth is paying for it, too, by having to absorb the waste.

▶ **4** Recycle packaging whenever you can. Reuse the plastic bags used to weigh fruits and vegetables by using them on the next trip to the market.

▶ **5** Encourage manufacturers to market "refills." Yes, your suggestion letters are read! We're already beginning to see it happen with a leading fabric softener. Juice companies have been doing it for years with their frozen and boxed concentrates.

▶ **6** Whenever possible buy returnable bottles and cans. If you can't, set aside space and collect them until you have enough to cart to a recycling center. Have your child sort (into brown, clear, and green), rinse the insides, and remove the labels.

▶ **7** Encourage your children to collect the stray bottles and cans they see on their outdoor excursions. It not only supports the recycling effort, it helps keep public areas clean.

▶ **8** Buy in bulk. Many supermarkets are now offering a bulk foods section where you can buy everything from spices and candy to pet food, pasta, cookies, and much more. If you empty your purchases into reusable containers at home, you can bring the plastic bags back to the store for refilling on your next shopping trip. And besides, your kids will love filling, weighing, and labeling the bags.

Talk to them about why buying in bulk is a preferable choice to buying prepackaged goods: You only buy the quantity you need and avoid having to dispose of excess packaging, creating a lot less waste all around.

PAPER OR PLASTIC?

"Paper or plastic?"—the first words uttered by a grocery check-out clerk, and a no-win proposition for the consumer. At first glance it seems a simple enough decision—paper is a renewable resource and biodegradable, plastic is not. True enough. But the problem with paper bags is that they are made out of 100 percent virgin paper. Recycled paper does not have the strength to bear the weight of a full bag of groceries. Oddly enough, the production process of paper bags is more environmentally hazardous than the production of plastic bags. Large amounts of toxins are spewed into the air and released in waste water. On the flip side, when plastic is burned—and about 10 percent of our trash *is* burned—noxious chemicals are similarly released.

make a difference!

▶ Don't accept any bags at all. Bring your own. There are any number of alternatives available to you.

- Make a heavy canvas bag of your own. Have your child decorate it with nonsoluble fabric paints. Paint pictures of fruit, vegetables, and your favorite grocery items.
- For those of you with a European grandmother, remember the expandable string bags she used to carry her groceries? They're back! You can purchase them by contacting mail-order companies listed in Chapter 5.
- Encourage your child's participation by buying or making a smaller version for her use.
- Don't limit yourself to using specially marketed bags to do your shopping. You can use any kind of heavy-duty bag. Some environmentally conscious shoppers even use the lighter, smaller pieces of luggage that otherwise sit in their attics waiting to be filled on the yearly family vacation. Why not make use of them in between?

Using your own bags, whether it's one recycled from a previous shopping trip or something practical but out-of-the-ordinary, you will meet with all kinds of reactions from store clerks. Some will be pleased, some will look at you with a raised eyebrow, and some will come right out and ask you where you found such a clever alternative. Be willing to share your information. And be willing to complain when you don't feel that your important consumer voice is being listened to. If you shop at a store where plastic is the only option, make your voice heard by the management. Insist on environmentally safe choices.

DON'T BE SHY!
HOW TO COMPLAIN ABOUT
FOOD PRODUCTS

You can do it. Apart from the packaging issue, you have the right to insist on quality food products for you and your family. In many ways, you have little right to complain about them if you don't exercise your consumer voice. Some store managers will listen to your verbal complaints and respond with action. But by far the most effective tactic is to return an unsatisfactory item to the store from which it was purchased, and follow up with a letter of complaint to the manufacturer (sending a copy to the store). No company wants to endure the unpleasantness of bad PR and the possibility of a boycott. Consult Appendix 3 for letter-writing suggestions.

make a difference!
▶ 1 Check the product label for the offending company's name, city, state, and zip code. These are quite often sufficient to use as an address. Most large manufacturing companies have a consumer affairs division. By doing a little extra homework, you can generally find this address as well as a contact name. It's good to know that your complaint has reached an actual pair of "ears."
   • In a letter, state your complaint clearly. Attach the Universal Product Code (UPC) symbol (the black bar code now found on all grocery store items) as a proof of purchase.

State the type of compensation you prefer (if you have not already been reimbursed by the store), whether it be a refund, coupons, or a replacement item, and be sure to include your return address.

• Keep a copy of the correspondence. If you do not hear back from the company within a reasonable length of time, send a second copy of the letter, noting that this is indeed the second copy.

Seldom are these letters ignored. Often you will receive coupons for free items, a replacement of the product itself, and always a letter of acknowledgment, generally in the form of an apology. Remember, you are providing these companies with an invaluable service. They pay consulting firms millions of dollars to test market their products. Your letter offers valuable feedback free of charge.

▶ **2** For the truly committed, consult *Shopping for a Better World* (discussed in Chapter 5). It will help you to determine which manufacturers you want to support, based on a number of political and environmental criteria. Pocket-sized, with an easy-to-read format, it allows you to decide at a glance whether the dishwashing liquid (or any other product) you buy contributes to the destruction of the environment, the political shame of South Africa, or the testing of animals, among several other considerations. For a copy, contact:

The Council on Economic Priorities
30 Irving Pl.
New York, NY 10003

▶ **3** If you are a concerned consumer who wants to keep abreast of food developments, there is an organization designed to help you do just that. The Center for Science in the Public Interest is a nonprofit, educational organization dedicated to the support of safe foods and accurate labeling procedures. The CSPI publishes a monthly *Nutrition Action Newsletter* with a section devoted to "Food Porn" (new products that don't make the grade) and "The Right Stuff" (new products that receive acknowledgment as healthy choices for you and your family). For more information, contact the Center for Science in the Public Interest:

CSPI
1501 16th St., N.W.
Washington, D.C. 20009

Now what? You and your child have shopped responsibly, choosing environmentally minded packaging and organic produce; you've brought your own shopping bag; you've stayed away from additives, pesticides, plastics, and steered clear of manufacturers who don't have an environmental bone in their collective body. But your kids are *still* asking for a plastic bag of something crunchy (and it *still* isn't Brazil nuts). You've talked to them about health, nutrition, food and the environment, food and the economy, food and the importance of good eating habits . . . but no matter what you do, they still want junk, and shake their heads in disgust at the thought of a lentil. Well, okay . . . the occasional potato chip won't kill them, especially if you buy organically grown and processed potato chips. But you believe in the principles contained in all the new knowledge you've gained and you want your children to believe in them, too. Right? Then help them by increasing their level of involvement in what they eat.

As with all other suggestions in this book for teaching children to respect and care for the planet and their fellow humans, being involved in one of the more basic interrelationships with the planet—sharing its bounty—is essential. Children should be encouraged to take an interest in food. After all, they are curious about living things. Planting seeds, nurturing plants, and reaping the ultimate benefits of good health and responsibility teaches them to respect life and understand their connection to the world around them.

learning activities
From the time a child is small, food is a symbol of love and security. Eating food is a social activity, something to be enjoyed with friends and family. We want this experience to be as positive as possible. Adults can help by educating children to make good food choices, and by encouraging their participation in food preparation.

Listed below are a few projects designed to help you and your child with this task. They are meant to encourage the consumption of a variety of wholesome foods.

THE POLITICS OF FOOD

The first three activities are designed to help children explore the sights, sounds, smells, feel, and taste of food. Since all learning is done through one or more of the senses, food, appealing to *all* the senses, is a perfect medium.

▶ **1** On your next trip to the supermarket ask the children to find a food that is:

fuzzy (peach)	waxy (apple)
lumpy (broccoli)	seedy (strawberry)
sticky (dates)	soft (persimmon)
lacy (parsley)	hard (watermelon)

Use the same question to evaluate color: Ask them to find fruits or vegetables that are:

orange (carrots)	yellow (squash)
red (apples)	brown (potatoes)
green (lettuce)	white (cauliflower)
purple (eggplant)	blue (grapes)

Encourage the children to see the variations in color—the different apple colors, lettuce colors, grape colors, melon colors, etc. Have your child make the connection by examining the colors in a crayon box. Often the words used to describe a color will be related to a food, as in "mint green," "lemon yellow," and "blueberry blue."

▶ **2** Have them listen to the preparation of food and let them use their own words to describe it: chopping carrots and celery, squeezing oranges and lemons, grating cheese, popping corn, squishing garlic, shredding cabbage, sizzling fish on the grill—the combinations are endless.

▶ **3** After taste, food smells evoke the strongest sensory reaction. Use herbs and spices to bring this to life. Put small amounts in your hand and hold under the nose of a blindfolded child. Ask them to identify the smell. Tell them the name of the food if they don't know. Try cinnamon, ginger, oregano, cloves, basil, sage, curry, rosemary, dill, tarragon, anise, and others.

▶ **4** To demonstrate the incredible culinary diversity a particular food may have, pick one and experiment with a variety of recipes.

Apples are usually good for this project. Children trust the much-loved apple. If it can be made into so many wonderful treats, maybe broccoli can too. (Sure . . . sure!)

Apples can be made into juice, sauce, pie, cake, cider, vinegar, butter. They can be baked, dried, fried, or eaten raw in anything, from salads and puddings to cream sauces for roast chicken. Take a trip to an orchard this summer and show your children where apples actually come from. You may even be able to pick your own. In fact, investigate all the "pick your own" farms in your area. You'll find farms that offer beans, strawberries, melons, squash, and many other fresh fruits and vegetables.

▶ 5 Other things you can do? Make your own staple foods. You really don't have to buy these items at the store. The following are loose recipe guidelines for making your own staples. Ask your librarian or bookseller for a basic cookbook that will help you to refine the recipes.

• Make raisins from grapes. You'll need:

> seedless grapes
> a large bowl of water
> a paper plate
> cheesecloth

Wash the grapes thoroughly and set them one layer deep in the plate. Cover the plate with a piece of cheesecloth. Place the plate in direct sunlight away from dirt and dust. After at least four days, test the grapes by gently squeezing. If water still oozes out, leave them for one more day. Test again.

• Make butter from cream. You'll need:

> whipping cream
> a jar with a tight-fitting lid

Let the cream come to room temperature. Put in the jar, being careful not to drop it. Shake, shake, shake!

In a few minutes you'll have butter!

- Make yogurt from milk. You'll need:

    1 quart of skim milk
    a saucepan
    4 tablespoons of plain yogurt
    a bowl or a jar with a lid

    Heat the milk until warm. Add the yogurt culture. Put the mixture in the bowl, cover, and let stand for at least seven hours (or overnight) at room temperature. Refrigerate when it's done.

- Make cottage cheese from milk. To make one pound of cheese, you'll need:

    a 4-quart double-boiler
    a thermometer
    1 gallon of skim milk
    liquid rennet (a coagulating agent, available from
    health-food stores and food co-ops)
    a 4-quart bowl
    cheesecloth

    Heat water in the bottom part of the double-boiler to 80 degrees F. This is very important. Pour the milk into the top part of the double-boiler. Dilute three or four drops of rennet in a tablespoon of cold water and stir into the milk. Keep the milk at 80 degrees F. until it curdles. This will take between twelve and eighteen hours. You can put the milk in a warm oven overnight for this particular step. Place the curd in the cheesecloth and drain the excess liquid—the whey. When the cheese is almost firm, it is ready to eat. When the process is complete, make sure you refrigerate the cheese.

- Make peanut butter from peanuts. You'll need:

    1½ tablespoons oil (corn or peanut will do)
    a blender or a food processor
    about 1 cup unshelled roasted peanuts

Place the oil in the blender, and gradually add the shelled peanuts.

Grind the peanuts to the texture you want, creamy or crunchy.

- Make bread. In fact, make all of your baked goods—cookies, bagels, crackers, breadsticks, biscuits. There are any number of excellent baking books in your library and bookstore that can help you.
- Make ice cream. You'll need:

milk and cream or evaporated milk
sugar
flavorings such as fruits and nuts
a commercial ice-cream maker
rock salt if the machine is a hand-crank version

Mix your ingredients and add them to your machine. Follow manufacturer's guidelines. It's a relatively easy process that will give you the best-tasting ice cream.

- Make potato chips. You'll need:

potatoes with the skins left on (but wash them thoroughly)
oil for deep frying

Slice the potatoes into very thin slices. Deep-fry until golden brown. Drain off the excess fat.

- Make jam. You'll need:

your favorite fruit
a saucepan

You can make fresh jam each week. To make larger quantities you'll need to follow other procedures for cooking and storing. The simple version merely requires boiling fresh or canned fruit until the water evaporates and the natural sugars come out. Depending on the kind of fruit, you may need to add a little sugar as a coagulant.

• Make juice. You'll need:

oranges and a glass

Squeeze! Juice! For those with adventuresome tastes, more elaborate juicers are available that can even turn carrots into juice!

• Make noodles. You'll need:

2 eggs
2 cups flour
1 tablespoon oil
1 tablespoon water
a rolling pin

Combine the ingredients and roll out into the desired thickness on a floured surface. Cut into the desired lengths and widths and boil in water just until the noodles float to the top. If you want to be more creative, commercial pasta machines are available that can make many different shapes and sizes. Vegetables like spinach or tomatoes (in paste form) can be added to the dough for added color and flavor.

• Make a salad. These can be fun and colorful, and are a wonderful way to introduce new vegetables—especially those from your own garden. Try these bright, flavorful ingredients: red, yellow, and green peppers, miniature corn, cherry tomatoes, peas in their pods, various kinds of squash and lettuce, radishes, and beets.

▶ 6 Have your children create recipe cards for each cooking experiment. Their favorites can be put into a notebook, or they can create a vegetable cookbook of their own.

Show your child that not everything we like to eat comes out of a box. There are many wonderful foods we can make ourselves. Special treats are right there in your kitchen, waiting to be created. (The children will, of course, need your initial help with many of these tasks.) Your library and bookstore are full of books to show you how.

By making or growing your own, you have the satisfaction of controlling (to a larger extent) what goes into and what stays out of your food, and you have the added bonus of eliminating the waste of excess packaging. Try it!

outdoor education

A child is a person who is going to carry on what you have started. The fate of humanity is in his hands. So it might be well to pay him some attention.

Abraham Lincoln

THIS book is about preparing the next generation to assume the responsibility for a fragile planet. Common sense dictates that if we are to take this responsibility seriously, we must prepare our children from an early age. Doing so gives them an added boost of commitment and the understanding necessary to assume the task. You do not have to work alone in this preparatory stage. Your level of commitment can be demonstrated by initiating any number of simple activities, and augmented by more involved organizational programs. There are even entire schools dedicated to helping young people learn about and understand the human relationship to the natural world.

"Outdoor education" can be something as simple as a walk in the woods. It can be an overnight stay at an outdoor school or a two-week wilderness trek in a national park. It can be full-time attendance at a specially designed "outdoor" school, where human relationship to the environment is the focal point. Regardless of the lengths you wish to go—as a parent, an educator, or a young person—you must examine your priorities and determine the most reasonable course for your own lifestyle.

A motivated, educated adult can help tremendously in motivating and educating a young person. In order to develop understanding, compassion, and an ethical relationship with our planet, kids need hands-on, multisensory experiences. Simply passing along the vocabulary is not enough. It's easy to become a "spectator" in this high-stress age we live in. It's easy to disavow any real responsibility for the state of the Earth when the problems loom so large. But when you look into the faces of your children, the need to do something to help the environment becomes a little stronger, a little more pressing. They deserve your involvement.

Even if you feel that "saving the planet" is too abstract and not motivation enough, consider the emotional and spiritual benefits of nature, the outdoor classroom. Few people can deny the absolute peace they feel out in the woods, or walking in a meadow, or breathing the tangy sea air. Nature has much to teach us, and many gifts to bestow upon us. How do we learn about them?

OUTDOOR SCHOOLS

Outdoor schools are a relatively new concept in Western education. They are institutions committed to teaching adults and children about the Earth and our relationship to it by allowing them to experience nature firsthand (Native Americans, of course, have been doing this for centuries). The philosophy of an outdoor school centers on the fact that primary, hands-on knowledge is much more powerful than reading a science textbook in an urban classroom or passively exploring the natural world on television (though these activities certainly have their place and value).

Programs at outdoor schools vary in length from just a few days to several weeks, and year-long study programs are available for older students. There is a great variety of classes to choose from. You can observe wildflowers where they grow, take rafting trips, study geology among the rocks, examine an actual glacier, help with bird banding, and that's just the beginning. A number of these schools operate on public lands. The Teton Science School, a twenty-three-year-old private and nonprofit science education center, for example, operates a campus inside the Grand Teton National Park in Wyoming. The National Park Service granted the school the rights to an old dude ranch made up of twenty-seven rustic buildings, one of which serves as a laboratory with computers and a telescope for stargazing. With access to over 10 million acres of the incredible Grand Teton and Yellowstone National parks, as well as to the Shoshone National Forest, the students (whose ages range from ten to senior adulthood) spend 80 percent of their time in these magnificent outdoor areas taking in and learning about their surroundings, and how they fit into the natural order. Classes last anywhere from a couple of days to several weeks.

Below you will find a list of some of the more popular and well-known outdoor schools in the country. The list will continue to grow as more and more educators and citizens feel the need to make a deeper connection to the natural world. Feel free to write or call for information. An outdoor school in your area may be a prospective vacation spot.

Ananda How-to-Live Schools
14618 Tyler Foote Rd.
Nevada City, CA 95959

Canyonlands Field Institute
P.O. Box 68
Moab, UT 84532
801-259-7750

Colorado Outdoor Education
Center
The Nature Place
Florissant, CO 80816
719-748-3341

Four Corners School of Outdoor Recreation
East Route
Monticello, UT 84535
800-525-4456

The Glacier Institute
P.O. Box 1457B
Kalispell, MT 59903

Hancock Field Station
John Day Fossil Beds
Fossil, OR 97830
503-763-4691

The Hobe Sound Nature Center, Inc.
P.O. Box 214
Hobe Sound, FL 33475
407-546-2067

Keystone Science School
Box 606
Keystone, CO 80435
303-468-5824

National Outdoor Leadership School
P.O. Box AA
Lander, WY 82520
307-332-2794

North Cascades Institute
2105 Highway 20
Sedro Wooley, WA 98284
206-856-5700

Olympic Park Institute
HC Box 9T
Port Angeles, WA 98362
206-928-3720

Outward Bound USA
384 Field Point Rd.
Greenwich, CT 06830
203-661-0797

Pocono Environmental Education Center
R.D. 2
Box 1010
Dingmans Ferry, PA 18328
717-828-2319

Point Reyes Field Seminars
Point Reyes, CA 94956
415-663-1200

Rocky Mountain Seminars
Rocky Mountain National Park
Estes Park, CO 80517
303-586-2371

Teton Science School
P.O. Box 68W
Kelly, WY 83011
301-733-4765

The Yellowstone Institute
Box 117
Yellowstone National Park, WY 82190
307-344-7381, ext. 2384

Yosemite Field Seminars
Yosemite Association
P.O. Box 230
El Portal, CA 95318
209-379-2646

Yosemite Institute
P.O. Box 487
Yosemite, CA 95318
209-372-4441

make a difference!

▶ **1** Consult your local phone book under "Parks and Recreation" to find out if a nature center, a bike or nature trail, camps, arboretums, or specific outdoor education programs can be found in your area. Local programs are usually free, supported by your tax dollars, and brochures are generally available upon request.

▶ **2** Call the Department of Education in your area and find out about outdoor education in your local schools. Your school district probably has access to an outdoor school or an outdoor laboratory. These are often operated and funded in part by community volunteers. Why not be a volunteer? It's a great way to get you and your child involved.

- Several nonprofit organizations have developed excellent environmental materials and make them available to teachers, parents, and students. The material generally provides lessons that can be taught in the classroom or at home. (See Chapter 9 under "Other Educational Materials.")

- Encourage your schools and parks to offer after-school programs (if they are not already available) in gardening, nature walks, geology, lepidopterology (the study of butterflies), etc. Offer to teach one!

▶ **3** Take an outdoor family vacation. Ecotourism is a great form of family-centered environmental education. We'll discuss this further in the following chapter.

▶ **4** Adopt a park, trail, camp, or beach area. Make a commitment to have an annual family picnic and "pickup" day. Spend an hour or two after the meal cleaning up the area before you leave. Make it your goal to leave the area cleaner than when you arrived. Collect any recyclable items that can be brought home and taken to the recycling center, rather than disposing of them in public receptacles. Family traditions of this sort can evoke wonderful memories and reaffirm commitments.

- In many outdoor tourist areas, organized cleanup days are scheduled by community activists or clubs at the end of the season. Cleanup days are easy to manage with kids and provide an opportunity to become involved with local environmental groups.

▶ **5** Encourage your child's participation in outdoor education programs, camps, or organizations such as Scouting or 4-H. An open-minded, supportive, and willing parent is all it takes. If you don't have a lot of spare time, your child's interest can blossom without you as long as the doors are open.

▶ **6** Make your message clear and consistent. Avoid confusion and conflict by setting an appropriate example. For instance, if your child sees you toss a paper napkin out of the car window, even though you preach recycling at home, a confusing message will be sent. We can't practice good ecological habits "sometimes." If we take the family camping and use paper plates and cups the message will again be blurred. It's no harder to wash dishes on a camping trip than it is at home. Old habits are not easy to change, but change is important.

▶ **7** Read to your child. You don't have to be outdoors to benefit from outdoor education. There is a vast array of nature books available that offer a wealth of information ranging from nature stories and games, craft projects and interpretive color books, to science-oriented explorations of the natural world. You can find materials at the local library, nature center, aquarium, zoo, and park visitor center, or order them from specialty stores, mail-order catalogs, and from any number of national and international environmental organizations.

- Use the resource chapter of this book to help you make decisions about reading material, but remember, hundreds of new books are published every year, and a number of them are about nature and the environment. Keep your eyes open for titles of interest, and encourage your child to choose these books in the library.

▶ **8** Contact organizations specializing in outdoor education and find out what's available near you. Price, length of the program, and student age will differ according to the focus of the different programs. You'll find that many programs are designed for adults. A wilderness experience may be the very jolt you need to motivate you to act. For more information about these schools and their offerings, contact the:

North American Association for Environmental Education
Dept. A
P.O. Box 400
Troy, OH 45373

The Sierra Club can also provide you with information about these kinds of programs.

▶ **9** Financially support environmental groups. Your donation is tax-deductible and it will usually entitle you to membership and special outdoor education programs and outings. Many of these groups will be happy to have you along even if you do not become a member.

AT SCHOOL

Even if your child can't attend an outdoor school, or there aren't any "nature centers" in your area, there are changes you can make at your child's school to help the environment. Get together with the parent-teacher association (PTA) and discuss the environmental goals parents and teachers can accomplish together.

A good way to begin is by organizing an Environmental Committee of the PTA. Its objective should be to ensure that the school your child attends makes environmental awareness and responsibility a priority for teachers, students, and parents. Here are some areas on which you can focus:

▶ **1** Encourage environmental issues to be a featured part of the curriculum at every grade level, and have books with an environmental focus available for every grade level in the library.

▶ **2** Encourage the expansion of bus routes so that all children will be able to use the system and cars can remain at home. When this is not possible, organize car pools.

▶ **3** Consider planting a vegetable garden to help provide fresh nutritious produce for school lunches and snacks. Each class can start a particular crop in the classroom and transfer it to the garden during the appropriate time. A maintenance schedule can be arranged so that each class will have an opportunity to work in the garden. Encourage the use of organic, not chemical, gardening methods.

▶ **4** Encourage the "Three Rs"—Reduce, Reuse, and Recycle. In most schools there is much that can be done in this area.

- The Styrofoam food trays and plastic utensils used in many schools should be abolished in favor of washable, reusable dishes and utensils.
- Recycling bins should be set up in the school cafeteria—one for compostable garbage (uneaten food items), one for cans,

one for glass, and one for paper. Children should be instructed in the use of these receptacles and encouraged to do so.

- Rather than throw away uneaten lunchbox goodies, a "swap table" can be provided. This will encourage children to share food they are not going to eat rather than waste it.
- Paper recycling should be instituted in the classroom as a daily practice. Parents can volunteer to transport the paper to recycling centers or, if enough accumulates, pickup can be arranged.
- Every classroom should have a box for recyclable paper. Teachers should be encouraged to reuse paper so that both sides are used before disposal.

▶ 5 Ensure that your school is tested for radon and asbestos levels (the latter is a requirement of the Environmental Protection Agency's Toxic Substance Control Act).

▶ 6 Make sure that lead levels are checked in the drinking water supply.

▶ 7 Encourage school use of the same water-saving devices as described for home use: toilet dams, low-flow shower heads, faucet aerators, etc.

▶ 8 Encourage your child's school to practice the same kinds of energy-saving habits that you do in your own home: turning off the lights when not in use, keeping air-conditioning/heating equipment well-maintained, and setting temperatures at a reasonable level.

learning activities

▶ 1 Take a nature walk with your children. Bring along some colored pencils or crayons, a sketch pad, a magnifying glass, and some binoculars if you have them. Relax and be patient; structure and time schedules are not as important as the adventure and thrill of discovery. Try some of the following activities:

- Together, draw pictures of things that please you. Sketch a flower, leaf, tree branch, or spider web laced with dew.
- Be a bird- or insect-watcher. Describe the size, feeding habits, markings, songs, flight, and other interesting behaviors of the critter.
- Make a rubbing. Place a piece of paper on a large rock, tree trunk, or over a leaf. With the flat side of an unpapered

crayon, rub and feel the texture of the object as it appears on your paper.

- Look for animal tracks or—ever-popular with kids—animal droppings. If you're ambitious, bring along some plaster of paris to make molds of the tracks you find. You can later compare and identify the tracks of different animals.
- Take this opportunity to talk about habitats, sensitizing your child to the needs of living things. It's endlessly fascinating to see how plants and animals obtain their basic needs of food, air, water, a suitable temperature, and living space. There's no right or wrong to this activity; simply pay attention to what your child finds and encourage the exploration and discussion.
- You can encourage the creative talents of older children by having them bring along their camera, musical instrument, writing journal, poetry, or watercolors and charcoal. Many famous creative artists like Ansel Adams and Henry Thoreau found their inspiration outdoors.

Before taking your educational walk in the woods, consider the following tips:

- Learn to recognize poison oak and poison ivy. Avoid plants with three shiny leaves per stem. Don't hesitate to point them out whenever you see them. Wearing long pants will help protect against these poisonous plants—and thorns and insects, too.
- Carry a light backpack with supplies. Include a water bottle, sweater, bag or cup to collect treasures, and some snacks. Keep collecting to a minimum. *Never* take a specimen of something that is rare or endangered in the area. Teach your child the ethical issue: Look and enjoy, but leave it for others to enjoy, too.
- Gauge the distance of your walk to your child's ability.
- Avoid places that may frighten small children. Areas with deep brush or requiring steep climbs may overwhelm a child.
- If nature calls while you are outdoors and a toilet is not available, teach your child to find a private spot off the trail and well away from any stream or spring. Scatter dirt, leaves, or rocks over the area, leaving it as close as possible to the way you found it.

▶ **2** Plan trips to the zoo, aquariums, fish farms, museums, and planetariums. Consider the advantages of membership: Special educational opportunities are often available to those who financially support these institutions.

▶ **3** Organize a family stargazing night. Drive away from the city lights and bring along a constellation chart, blanket, and some munchies. If planning the real thing becomes too involved, audiovisual products are available that will shine a map of the universe on your ceiling and help you to identify the planets and constellations in the privacy of your own home. The thrill of an actual excursion, however, will always be remembered and cherished.

For more information about star kits, contact:

Bushnell
A Division of Bausch & Lomb
300 N. Lone Hill Ave.
San Dimas, CA 91773

▶ **4** Make a trip into the wilderness. Start with a simple camping trip or cross-country ski expedition, and progress from there to more advanced backpacking adventures.

▶ **5** Orienteering is an exciting subject to explore with an older child. Using a compass and a topographic map, plot out some short, simple trails and follow them to your destination. Treasure hunts in your backyard can be fun, too. Dad or mom can plot out a map beforehand, plant the treasure, and provide the clues: "Twelve paces north and twenty paces northeast," and so on, eventually leading the kids to the "X" spot where the treasure is hidden. (If you are not familiar with orienteering skills, leave this subject to an outdoor school rather than risking the loss of your family in the wilderness!)

▶ **6** Interest even your youngest children in simple crafts or nature projects. For instance, rolling a pinecone in peanut butter and bird seed is a simple project for any child. Tie a string to the pinecone and suspend it from a tree to encourage birds to feed in your yard. Point out the different species with their distinctive colors and markings.

▶ **7** Consider purchasing a copy of Joseph Cornell's *Sharing Na-*

ture with Children and his *Sharing the Joy of Nature—Nature Activities for All Ages.*

Joseph Cornell is one of the world's preeminent nature educators. His outdoor workshops, which focus on nature awareness, have attracted thousands of adults and children from many countries. Cornell has developed a series of nature "games" and activities designed to stimulate an awareness of the peace, beauty, and energy found in the natural world. His teaching methods are based on the philosophy that one should:

- Share rather than teach by imparting personal feelings about each species of tree, animal, flower, element, etc. Sharing your feelings encourages children to explore their own.
- Be open and receptive. Every question a child asks is important. Respect your child's mood, and be alert to what causes his curiosity to be aroused.
- Focus on the child's interests and immediately set the child's attention on those interests during an outing. If trees hold some special interest for your child, focus on trees.
- Experience first and discuss later. Children do not often forget a lesson taught by direct experience. Words, whether read or heard, are much more easily forgotten.
- Make it fun! The joy of nature is infectious and should be shared with enthusiasm.

You may be wondering what form these games and activities take. Here are three examples from Cornell's books.

- *Heartbeat*

Find a sturdy deciduous tree (coniferous, or "evergreens," do not work as well), preferably in early spring when the tree's sap is running. The tree trunk should be at least 6 inches in diameter.

Place a stethoscope firmly on the trunk, making sure that you do not create unnatural noises by moving it or yourself. It may take several attempts to find the right spot.

You should be able to hear the sound of early sap rising through the trunk just as the blood flows through our bodies.

Let your child listen to the sound of his own heartbeat and

maybe that of a cooperative family pet. All living things have a "heartbeat."

• *Recipe for a Forest*

Give your child an imaginary plot of land on which to create the forest of his choice.

On a piece of paper, have him list all the ingredients that make up his forest—all the animals, birds, trees, water sources, weather patterns, etc.

Encourage him to discuss and plan out every aspect of the forest, including soil and air conditions. Help him to discover the various components.

After you've discussed the "recipe," have him draw a picture (the bigger the better) of his forest with as much detail and using as much variety of color as possible.

• *Still-hunting*
American Indians used still-hunting as a means to learn about and observe nature. A brave would seek out a place he knew or was attracted to. There he would sit and let his mind relax and become still. If his sudden appearance caused the animals to become agitated, he would wait quietly until they resumed their normal behavior. There he would watch, and learn.

Take your child still-hunting. Let him find a place that he feels attracted to. It may be near a tree, a water source, or out in an open field. Whatever the case, let him choose.

Instruct him to be as quiet as possible. The purpose of this exercise is to watch, blending in with your surroundings. Choose your own spot to still-hunt.

Talk to him about what he has heard and seen. Share your experiences as well. Share your feelings, and encourage him to verbalize his.

▶ 8 Encourage your children to write or call the environmental organizations listed in the resource chapter of this book for further information about nature and environmental issues. Don't do it for them. It is an excellent exercise, not only in the art of letter writing, but in learning what to ask for and how to ask for it. Almost all the environmental groups listed have an educational program or materials of some sort and are more than happy to respond to young letter writers. Here are some guidelines to follow for writing these letters. (For more information on effective letter writing, please see Appendix 3.)

- Address your correspondence (if you do not have the name of a staff member) to the "Public Information Office," the "Education Office," or the "Community Affairs Office."
- Include your name and complete address in the letter so that you will be assured of a reply.
- State your request simply and don't ask for too much all at once.
- It is a good idea to include a self-addressed stamped envelope with your request. It may expedite the delivery of the return information, and it is an added way of supporting the organization because it does not have to pay for postage.
- Be very patient. Many of these organizations are understaffed or make use of volunteers who only work on a part-time basis. It may take some time for them to respond.
- Share any information you receive with your friends, family, and classmates. Spread the word!

▶ 9 Write up a pollution pledge: Written contracts are effective visual commitments. Children enjoy writing down their chosen responsibilities and are more likely to want to fulfill this kind of obligation.

- Start with the basics: I,_____, pledge to help the Earth by . . .

Some suggestions to complete this sentence include:

> turning out the lights when I leave the room;
> rinsing out containers and putting them in the right place for recycling;
> reusing old toys or giving them to someone else to reuse;
> hanging laundry;

riding my bike instead of asking my Mom or Dad to drive me somewhere;
watching only one hour of television a day;
using both sides of the paper when I color;
feeding the birds.

- Let him choose which activities he wants to focus on in his pledge. There are many ways he can help. Once the pledge is written, have him sign it, with you as a witness.
- This is an excellent activity for every member of the family. We should all make the pledge to help the Earth.

Parents who influence and teach their children to "walk lightly on the Earth" deserve a debt of gratitude from society. Those children who have the opportunity to grow up with an outdoor classroom learn to "connect the dots" of interrelated environmental issues at an early age. Sharing nature activities brings all of us closer to the Earth and makes us feel more a part of the complete natural process, not just the isolated, dominant creatures many of us think we are.

Home efforts to turn out the lights, compost the eggshells, and recycle the waste will take on meaning as your child begins to understand and combine his experiential outdoor understanding of the Earth with his knowledge about the more pragmatic aspects of environmental education.

eco-
tourism

Everybody needs beauty as well as bread, places to play in, where nature may heal and give strength to body and soul.

John Muir

TOURISM is the third-largest industry in the world, and one of the fastest-growing. Traveling to new places takes us away from what we know and puts us into the exciting adventure of discovering what we do not know about this planet of ours. It is an exhilarating, eye-opening, educational experience for adults and children alike.

An increasing number of travelers, and tour companies, are flocking to countries that have only recently discovered the positive impact of the tourist trade. Often these countries have little else to depend on for economic gain: They are poor, underdeveloped, and lacking in viable resources, except for one—their natural environments.

The traveling public is looking for the exotic, the remote, the pristine—conditions found in many of the less developed countries of Asia and Africa. Unfortunately, thought is seldom given to the potential damage a heavy influx of people may have on these fragile areas. The result is that the pristine environments that attracted tourism in the first place often become so overburdened that they deteriorate, and the country is then no longer able to sustain its tourist trade *or* its environment.

The same holds true for domestic travel. In our search for wilderness and wildlife, do we ever stop to think what effect our presence will have in these areas? We should.

issue

In remote areas, airports are being built and villages dismantled—and rarely relocated—to accommodate new hotels and resorts. Vessels are discharging waste as they travel through our oceans and waterways.

Acknowledging the need for a more responsible approach to traveling, a new trend is emerging in the travel industry—"ecotourism." An offshoot of the "adventure travel" of the past two decades, ecotourism mixes the excitement of visiting exotic, wild locations, with consideration for the political and environmental impact of human travel. It is by no means a solution to what could become a significant environmental problem, but it does serve to a certain extent as "preventive medicine."

TRAVEL ETHIC

As a means of providing some standards for the industry, the National Audubon Society has developed a travel ethic which it encourages the travel industry and private individuals to adopt. Its directives are simple, but if you and your family follow them, your impact on the natural areas you visit will be lessened. Only by respecting and protecting these natural areas can we ensure their presence for future generations to enjoy.

▶ **1** *Wildlife and their habitats must not be disturbed.*
Wildlife includes *all* plants and animals. We have already discussed the important roles that plants play in the environment. Wild plants should never be removed, their flowers picked, or their leaves

disturbed. This is true for wild vegetation on land and in water. With respect to animals, their behavior should never be dictated by human behavior. When out among them, *you* are the visitor in *their* home. They should not feel frightened or threatened by your presence. Any time and energy that an animal must spend defending its territory or young from humans is time and energy taken away from its natural function on Earth. There are several points to remember when it comes to wildlife, and they should be shared with your children:

- Animals, whether alone or in a group, should never be surrounded.
- Visitors should never come between animal parents and their young.
- Visitors should never come between water mammals and the water—for example, seals and the water's edge.
- Nesting raptors (eagles, hawks, etc.) should only be watched from a distance through binoculars or a telescope.
- Do not touch or "bother" animals in any way, just to get a good photograph.

▶ **2** *Tourism to natural areas will be sustainable.*
Individuals involved in any aspect of managing a tourist area are encouraged to develop long-term visitor plans to ensure that these areas will continue to exist in the future.

▶ **3** *Waste disposal during travel must have neither environmental nor aesthetic impact.*
Tourist sites must be kept as clean as possible. Any trash made or seen at a site should come home with you and disposed of properly. This applies to water travel as well. Never dump anything over the side of a boat or ship.

▶ **4** *The experience a tourist gains in traveling must enrich his/her appreciation of nature, conservation, and the environment.*
Tours should be led by experienced guides and naturalists who are well-acquainted with the flora and fauna of the area you are visiting. They should be able to answer your questions and encourage your appreciation of the site.

▶ **5** *Tours must strengthen the conservation effort and enhance the natural integrity of places visited.*
Local conservation group representatives should be encouraged to

share their knowledge of local conservation efforts as a means of educating visitors about the global nature of environmental concerns.

▶ **6** *Traffic in products that threaten wildlife and plant populations must not occur.*

Pay strict attention to the kinds of "souvenirs" you buy. Many items manufactured abroad are created at great cost—the loss of indigenous animal life. Whether at home or on vacation, please do not buy:

- any products derived from sea turtles such as tortoiseshell jewelry, turtle meat and eggs, and certain skin creams;
- most reptile skins, especially those from Latin America, China, the Caribbean, and Egypt;
- snakeskin products from Latin America and Asian countries;
- anteater leather from Indonesia, Thailand, and Malaysia;
- ivory, especially from elephants and marine mammals such as whales and walruses;
- birds (including feathers and skins) from Latin America, Australia, and the Caribbean;
- coral from the Caribbean and Southeast Asia;
- any fur or fur products;
- any orchids or cacti.

▶ **7** *The sensibilities of other cultures must be respected.*

When we travel to other countries, we are guests of those countries and their people. We are there to learn and share, not to criticize and disregard their ways and customs.

Adhering to these guidelines as they apply to individuals, and supporting tour companies that comply with the travel ethics in general, will only strengthen the conservation aspect of traveling. Doing so fosters respect for the planet and all her creatures. Consider your vacation a privilege extended by the Earth and keep to the standards outlined above. It is an important step in ensuring that your child learns to respect the partnership human beings should have with all other living things.

There are a couple of other points to remember about ecotravel. Nature tours are generally much less glamorous than standard tours to more common destinations. You'll often be faced with rustic accommodations, trails that are difficult to negotiate, especially after heavy rains, and services that are much less refined than what you have become accustomed to with other tours. But, then, your reasons for participating in a trip of this sort are different as well. To experience nature at close range requires that you put yourself in the midst of it. This is an important point to bear in mind if you wish to travel with your child. Make sure you consult the tour companies for the age guidelines recommended for their trips, and be sure to ask for tours specifically geared to families.

CHOOSING A RESPONSIBLE TOUR COMPANY

There are several factors to bear in mind when choosing an eco-tourism company.

- *Experience.* A tour company should have established contacts in the countries they visit, be well-organized with appropriate contingency plans, and have "thought of everything."
- *Commitment.* You need to feel certain that a company is truly dedicated to environmental concerns. Many of them even donate a portion of their proceeds to environmental organizations.
- *Training.* In-country as well as tour-company guides should be a part of the journey. The guides should be familiar with, hopefully fluent in, the local language, have lived in the area for a reasonable length of time, and be well-acquainted with the environmental concerns of the area.
- *Information.* You should expect to be given well in advance of your journey a complete itinerary, a list of necessary equipment, reading lists about the country or countries you'll be visiting, immunization requirements, etc. When shopping for a tour, make sure you find out just what the company offers in the way of preparation.

Below is a list of tour companies that offer ecotours. When you contact them, be sure to ask for brochures describing trips suitable for families.

ECOTRAVEL COMPANIES

Above the Clouds Trekking
P.O. Box 398
Worcester, MA 01602
508-799-4499 or 800-233-4499

Specializes in treks to Nepal and South America, among others, and supports a number of relief operations through nonprofit funds.

Biological Journeys
1696 Ocean Dr.
McKinleyville, CA 95521
415-527-9622 or 800-548-7555

Offers direct involvement with marine wilderness areas. Included are natural history and small-group whale watching expeditions in New Zealand, Australia, Baja, Alaska, and the Galapagos.

Environmental Traveling Companions
Building C, Fort Mason
San Francisco, CA 94123
415-474-7662

Organizes trips for the disabled and disadvantaged. Trips include rafting, sea kayaking, cross-country skiing, and other wilderness adventures.

Far Horizons
P.O. Box 1529
16 Fern Lane
San Anselmo, CA 94960
415-457-4575

Offers trips to many locations, including Turkey, Kenya, the Yucatan, Belize, and more. The philosophy of Far Horizons is that a traveler must interact with the local cultures: eat and drink local foods and beverages, learn the language, and visit with native people in their homes.

International Expeditions
776 Independence Court
Birmingham, AL 35216
800-633-4734

Offers a number of ecologically oriented tours, closely adhering to ecotourism guidelines.

Overseas Adventure Travel
349 Broadway
Cambridge, MA 02139
800-221-0814   617-876-0533

An environmentally sensitive, well-established company, with many tours to Africa. Profits are often donated to the host country.

Pacific Whale Cruises
101 N. Kihei Rd.
Kihei, HI 96753
808-879-8811

Operates whale watching day trips from November through mid-April in Hawaii. All proceeds are donated to the Pacific Whale Foundation.

Peace Child Foundation
9502 Lee Highway
Fairfax, VA 22031
703-385-4494   800-275-7231

Peace Child brings together children and teenagers from the United States, the Soviet Union, and Latin America to create performances that depict the struggle to end war and global conflict in our time.

Sobek Expeditions
Mountain Travel Sobek
6420 Fairmount Ave.
El Cerrito, CA 94530
800-227-2384   415-527-8100

Offers many trips across the globe. Makes donations ranging between $250 and $500 per booking to Rainforest Action Network.

Victor Emanuel Nature Tours
Mountain Travel Sobek
6420 Fairmont Ave.
El Cerrito, CA 94530
800-227-2384   415-527-8100

Offers many birding and natural history tours worldwide, donating a portion of its profits to various conservation organizations.

Wilderness Travel
801 Allston Way
Berkeley, CA 94710
415-548-0420 or 800-247-6700

Offers wildlife/nature-oriented educational trips to increase awareness of preservation in Asia, Africa, Europe, and South America. Supports Earth Preservation Trust through booking fees and donations.

MEMBERSHIP ORGANIZATION TRAVEL OPPORTUNITIES

EarthWatch
P.O. Box 403
Watertown, MA 02272
617-926-8200

Sponsors a variety of scientific research projects to assist scientists in fieldwork. Various levels of expertise are accepted for these two- to six-week projects. Open to members.

National Audubon Society
950 Third Ave.
New York, NY 10022
212-832-3200

There are twenty-four domestic and international natural culture and natural history trips to choose from each year.

National Wildlife Federation
1400 16th St., N.W.
Washington, D.C. 20036-2266
202-797-6800

Organizes field trips to a number of international and domestic destinations, offers special wildlife camps just for kids, and holds conservation summits for educators and interested adults.

The Nature Conservancy
1815 N. Lynn St.
Arlington, VA 22209
703-841-5300

Organizes field trips to Latin America and throughout the United States with emphasis on rare and endangered plants and animals and their habitats. Each trip is guided by an experienced naturalist and Conservancy staff member.

Rails to Trails Conservancy
1400 16th St., N.W., #300
Washington, D.C. 20036
202-797-5400

When you participate in a bicycling vacation in the United States, Ireland, or the Caribbean, Travent Ltd. will donate 10 percent of the tour price to Rails to Trails, a nonprofit organization which converts abandoned railroad tracks to trails for public use.

Sierra Club
730 Polk St.
San Francisco, CA 94109
415-776-2211

Both service and adventure trips are offered. Whether you choose a trip to help rebuild a trail through the Grand Canyon, or a safari through Kenya, trips are led by experienced volunteers. Send $2.00 for a list of Sierra Club outings.

World Wildlife Fund Expeditions
1250 24th St., N.W.
Washington, D.C. 20037
202-293-4800

Organizes Latin American and African expeditions to destinations such as Ecuador and the Galapagos Islands as well as Asia, Australia, and the Arctic Circle. Local conservation experts and research specialists act as guides.

make a difference!

▶ **1** Support travel companies that support the environment with both their travel practices and a percentage of their profits.

▶ **2** Consider a "working" or "service" vacation. This type of "vacation" is one in which participants actually work at saving, restoring, researching, nurturing, discovering, and otherwise helping the planet. A leader in the field is EarthWatch, whose mission it is to "improve human understanding of the planet, the diversity of its inhabitants, and the processes which affect the quality of life on earth." EarthWatch offers exciting opportunities to participate in their mission all over the world. The Soviet Deep Ocean Survey, for example, entails spending one month aboard a Soviet Ship mapping the Pacific Ocean floor. A trip like this would cost you approximately $2,000, an all-inclusive price. If it seems low, it's because you will be *working*. Other trips include: studying orangutans in Borneo and koalas in Australia, teaching language to dolphins, and uncovering the origins of urban Europe in France. There are many more. Even if you have no experience as a naturalist, EarthWatch will welcome you as a volunteer. Remember, there are many opportunities for all age groups.

▶ **3** When you go on vacation, make sure you:
   • Turn off all appliances and lights, and lower the thermostat in winter or turn the air conditioner off in summer.
   • Have your newspaper delivery put on hold. It will save you from returning home to a pile of wilted newspapers on the front lawn, and save a few trees as well.

• Share with friends and neighbors any remaining perishable food in your refrigerator. You don't want to come home to a carton of milk that has turned into cheese.

• If you have a garden, invite your neighbors to pick the produce rather than have it go to waste.

▶ **4** If you are traveling by airplane:

• Consider bringing your own snacks. How often do we complain about the food served on airlines? Rather than go to the trouble of having it heated and ultimately wasted, bring foods you enjoy eating, are relatively easy to manage, and that will keep you and your child satisfied.

• Make your feelings about disposable utensils and dinnerware heard. Ask a flight attendant who the best person would be to direct your comments. Be positive and offer suggestions. There are many nonbreakable options that are not single-use.

▶ **5** Take advantage of the tourist sites in your own city. It will save you time, money, and the vast amounts of energy required to travel to distant lands. Did you ever stop to consider what all those people who come to visit your city find so interesting about it? Rediscover all the wonderful local attractions—the zoo, the parks, the museums, the historic buildings. Make it a point to go and visit the sites that attract out-of-town visitors. How many of us have lived in a place for years and chastised ourselves for not taking advantage of the very opportunities that attract visitors?

learning activities

▶ **1** Keep a written journal of your trip (have your child do the same) to augment your photographic and video records. A journal will heighten your sense of participation with the different cultures you experience and will certainly provide a more intimate perspective than photos alone. You'll enjoy reliving your trip years later through your own unique written observations.

• Make notations about the smells and sounds of a place. Note the colors, the tastes of the different foods, the sound of the language.

• Add sketches of new and unfamiliar sights to your journal.

▶ **2** Before you retire for the evening, spend a few moments with your child discussing all the "new" sights and sounds she experienced—the ones that are different from familiar "home" sights and sounds.

▶ **3** Plan a theme excursion. This could be as short as a day, or as long as two weeks. Try the following suggestions:

- Attend all the sporting events that come to town during a particular time period.
- Visit every museum in town and keep a journal of the wild and exotic new things you encounter.
- Visit every park within a certain radius of your hometown. Plan on having a family picnic in each one.
- Volunteer your time as a family for one of the environmental groups that has an office in your area.

The possibilities are endless. All you need to do is spend a little time investigating the various options available close to home. You don't have to get in the car and drive for hundreds of miles to find beauty and time for one another.

CAMPING

For those of you who like to go camping, there are a few points we'd like you to keep in mind when you are out enjoying the many beautiful wilderness areas across this land. No matter where you go, and what you do, human activity does have an impact on even the most rugged areas.

▶ **1** Remember that you are a guest of Mother Nature. When we visit the homes of friends and relatives we do our best to respect their wishes and ways of doing things. The same holds true when you visit Mother Earth. Help to keep her house clean, your noise to a minimum, and your habits from overburdening her.

▶ **2** Choose a campsite carefully. If possible, to prevent any expansion of the site, pick one that has already been used. Remember that the site should be at least 100 feet from a water source. Keep the area free of debris and never frighten any wildlife that may need to use the water.

▶ **3** Use proper equipment for your site and yourself. Heavy-soled boots can damage delicate terrain. Consider the light-soled hiking boots now available, or a simple pair of well-soled athletic shoes.

▶ **4** Use established toilet facilities whenever possible. When they are not, dig a hole several inches deep and at least 100 feet away from the camp, water supply, and trails. Cover it with soil, leaves, or stones when you are finished.

▶ **5** To prevent any contamination from soaps and detergents, wash clothes, dishes, or personal items at least 100 feet from the water source. Instead of going to the water, bring the water to you.

▶ **6** Stick to established trails when hiking through the woods. There is no point in destroying any more ground vegetation than is necessary. Trail maps are usually available from the park ranger.

▶ **7** Follow safety rules when building campfires. Keep it small and away from other trees, use only fallen, dead wood, and make sure it has cooled sufficiently before you retire for the evening.

▶ **8** Remove all refuse from the campsite. Bring it home with you and dispose of it properly, recycling all recyclables and disposing of the rest.

▶ **9** If you enjoy fishing, make certain you use lead-free fishing weights. Over five thousand waterfowl are poisoned each year from the weights used on fishing poles.

resources

for

parents

THE following list of organizations, magazines, books, computer networks, hotlines, and newsletters will help guide you and your family to the best sources of current information on the environmental issues that concern you. Your support of these groups and publications allows them to continue the vital work of searching for a cure for our ailing planet. We have also included a list of books specifically written for children. Following the description of some organizations is a list of the educational materials that are available.

ORGANIZATIONS

The Acid Rain Foundation, Inc.
1410 Varsity Dr.
Raleigh, N.C. 27606
919-828-9443

This nonprofit, international organization was founded to foster a greater understanding of the acid rain problem and to seek a viable solution. Its goals are to develop and raise the level of public awareness, to supply educational materials, and to support research. Membership is $25 per year and includes a quarterly publication, *The Acid Rain Update*.

African Wildlife Foundation
1717 Massachusetts Ave., N.W.
Washington, D.C. 20036
202-265-8393

The AWF works in over twenty African countries to help promote, establish, and support grassroots and institutional conservation and wildlife management programs. Its current emphasis is on educating Americans not to buy ivory. Membership is $15 per year and includes the quarterly newsletter *Wildlife News*.

American Association of Zoological Parks
Oglevay Park
Wheeling, WV 26003-1698
304-242-2160

Write to this association for further information about "adopting" animals. It includes a list of zoos that participate in animal adoption programs.

American Cetacean Society
P.O. Box 2639
San Pedro, CA 90731-0943
213-548-6279

This nonprofit volunteer organization works to protect dolphins and whales through research, conservation, and education. Membership is $25 per year and includes a subscription to the quarterly magazine *Whale Watcher* and the *Whale News* newsletter.

The American Forestry Association
1516 P St., N.W.
Washington, D.C. 20005
202-667-3300

A national citizens' organization, the AFA is dedicated to the maintenance and improvement of the health and value of trees and forests, and to educating Americans about the importance of forest conservation and tree planting. It sponsors a program called "Global Releaf" which encourages people to plant trees as an effective means of lowering the carbon dioxide levels in our air and beautifying our neighborhoods. Membership is $24 per year and includes the bimonthly *American Forests*.

American Rivers
801 Pennsylvania Ave., S.E., #303
Washington, D.C. 20003
202-547-6900

American Rivers is a nonprofit group working to protect and preserve our rivers and their landscapes. Membership is $20 per year and includes the quarterly newsletter *American Rivers*.

Center for Marine Conservation, Inc.
1725 DeSales St., N.W., Suite 500
Washington, D.C. 20036
202-429-5609

CMC, Inc., is dedicated to protecting marine wildlife and their habitats, and to conserving coastal and ocean resources. Membership is $20 per year and includes the quarterly newsletter *Marine Conservation News*, legislative updates, and "Action Alerts" informing the public about how they can help support marine conservation. Educational materials: *A Citizen's Guide to Plastics in the Ocean*; *Directory of Marine Education Resources* (a guide to organizations, publications, and sanctuaries); *Marine Debris Coloring Book*.

Center for Science in the Public Interest
1501 16th St., N.W.
Washington, D.C. 20036
202-332-9110

This group provides consumer information relating to nutrition and health. It sponsors the "Americans for Safe Food" project, which focuses on sustainable agriculture. Membership is $19.95 per year and includes ten yearly issues of *Nutrition Action Health Letter.*

Citizen's Clearinghouse for Hazardous Wastes
P.O. Box 6806
Falls Church, VA 22040
703-237-2249

Lois Gibbs, a victim of the Love Canal tragedy, founded this organization in 1981 to help grassroots organizations fight for environmental justice. It currently works with six thousand groups nationwide, providing technical support and written material. Membership is $25 per year and includes the bimonthly magazine *Everyone's Backyard.*

Clean Water Action Project
317 Pennsylvania Ave., S.E.
Washington, D.C. 20003
202-547-1196

The emphasis of this organization is placed on pesticide safety and groundwater protection. The landfill crisis and protecting our endangered natural resources are other concerns. Membership is $24 per year for individuals and $40 per year for organizations and includes the quarterly newsletter *Water Action News.*

Clean Water Fund
317 Pennsylvania Ave., S.E., 3rd Fl.
Washington, D.C. 20003
202-547-2312

The Clean Water Fund focuses on developing the grassroots strength of the environmental movement. Issues of primary concern include water pollution, toxic hazards, and protecting natural resources. Membership is $25 per year and includes the quarterly newsletter *Water Action News*.

Concern, Inc.
1794 Columbia Rd., N.W.
Washington, D.C. 20009
202-328-8160

Concern, Inc., provides environmental information for community action. Its goal is to help communities find solutions to environmental problems that threaten public health and the quality of life. Booklets on various issues such as pesticide use, drinking water, and household waste, among others, can be purchased for $3.00 each.

The Cousteau Society, Inc.
930 W. 21st St.
Norfolk, VA 23517
804-627-1144

Founded by the eminent environmentalist Jacques-Ives Cousteau, this group seeks to protect and improve the quality of life for this and future generations. Activities include research, books, lectures, television specials, and more. Membership is $20 for individuals and $28 for families and includes the bimonthly magazine *Calypso Log*. Children receive *Dolphin Log*.

Cultural Survival
11 Divinity Ave.
Cambridge, MA 02138
617-495-2562

An academic group affiliated with Harvard University, Cultural Survival works to import sustainably managed rain forest products to the United States. It acts as a consultant to businesses seeking to import rain forest woods and nuts for their own use. Membership is $25 per year and includes the *Cultural Survival Quarterly*.

Defenders of Wildlife
1244 19th St., N.W.
Washington, D.C. 20036
202-659-9510

The Defenders of Wildlife is dedicated to protecting wild plants and animals in their habitats, especially threatened or endangered native American species. It accomplishes this through education, litigation, and advocacy. Membership is $20 per year and includes the bimonthly magazine *Defenders*. It also publishes a number of educational newsletters, endangered species reports, and citizen action alerts.

Elsa Wild Animal Appeal
P.O. Box 4572
North Hollywood, CA 91617
818-761-8387

This organization is concerned with the preservation of wildlife, especially endangered species, through child education. Focusing on the eighteen-and-under age group, it develops and distributes educational materials and is involved in legislation. Yearly membership—$15.00 for adults, $7.50 for children, and $5.00 for senior citizens—includes a triannual subscription to *Born Free News* and a choice of wildlife kits for home or classroom use. Children also receive "Action Alerts" such as "Save the Whales" and "Elephant Ivory Bans" with suggestions and information about what they can do to help.

Environmental Action, Inc.
1525 New Hampshire Ave.
Washington, D.C. 20036
202-745-4870

EA, Inc., is a lobbying organization that works directly with citizens' groups toward the passage of strong environmental laws such as the Clean Air Act and Superfund. Membership is $20 per year and includes the bimonthly *Environmental Action Magazine.*

Environmental Defense Fund
1616 P St., N.W., Suite 200
Washington, D.C. 20036
202-387-3500

The EDF is composed of scientists, economists, and lawyers who defend the environment. Membership is $20 per year and includes the quarterly *EDF Newsletter.*

Environmental Policy Institute
The Oceanic Society
218 D St., S.E.
Washington, D.C. 20003
202-544-2600

This organization was established to promote the conservation, protection, and rational use of the Earth and her resources. It engages in lobbying efforts, public information, and litigation. Membership is $25 for individuals, and $15 for students, senior citizens, and low-income supporters. It includes the monthly magazine *Not Man Apart.*

The Fund for Animals, Inc.
200 W. 57th St.
New York, NY 10019
212-246-2096

This group was founded to help aid the relief, fear, pain, and suffering of wild and domestic animals. Membership is $20 for individuals, and $25 for families. It includes a newsletter and updates on legislation.

Global Tomorrow Coalition
1325 G St., N.W.
Washington, D.C. 20005
202-628-4016

The Coalition is a national alliance of groups and individuals working together to promote understanding of the global trends in development, population, environment, and resources. Its primary focus is on sustainable development. Membership is $35 per year ($15 for senior citizens) and includes the quarterly newsletter *InterAction*. Educational materials: Biological Diversity Education Packet; Marine Resources Education Packet; Population Education Packet; Tropical Forests (a teaching packet).

Greenpeace USA, Inc.
1436 U St., N.W.
Washington, D.C. 20009
202-462-1177

Greenpeace is dedicated to protecting and preserving the environment and the life it supports. Membership is $20 per year and includes the bimonthly magazine *Greenpeace*.

The Humane Society of the United States
2100 L St., N.W.
Washington, D.C. 20037
202-452-1100

The Humane Society offers resources to the general public. Subjects include animal control, cruelty investigation, publications, and humane education. Membership is $10 per year.

The Izaak Walton League of America, Inc.
1401 Wilson Blvd., Level B
Arlington, VA 22209
703-528-1818

This group focuses on the protection of the nation's land, water, and air resources. Membership is $20 per year and includes the quarterly magazine *Outdoor America*.

Kids Against Pollution
P.O. Box 775, High St.
Closter, NJ 07624
201-784-0668

This membership organization produces a newsletter in which kids can trade success stories about anti-pollution efforts. Membership is $15 per year and includes the newsletter and information packets.

National Arbor Day Foundation
100 Arbor Ave.
Nebraska City, NE 68410
402-474-5655

Dedicated to tree planting and conservation, NADF provides direction, technical assistance, and public recognition for urban and community forestry programs as well as materials and information to help cities plan their own Arbor Day celebrations. Packets for children are also available. Membership is $10 per year and includes the bimonthly newsletter *Arbor Day.*

National Audubon Society
950 Third Ave.
New York, NY 10022
212-832-3200

The National Audubon Society seeks to conserve native plants, animals, and their habitats; protect life from pollution, radiation, and toxic substances; find solutions to global problems involving the interaction of population, resources, and the environment; and promote rational strategies for renewable energy development. Membership is $30 per year and includes the bimonthly *Audubon Magazine.* Educational materials: *Nature with Children of All Ages,* The Massachusetts Audubon Society (a manual of nature activities for children).

National Geographic Society
17th & M Sts., N.W.
Washington, D.C. 20036
202-857-7000

The world's largest scientific and educational nonprofit organization focuses primarily on publishing magazines, books for children and adults, and atlases; producing television programs; supporting environmental research; and developing geography education programs for school children. Membership is $21 per year and includes the monthly magazine *National Geographic.* Educational materials: Educational Services Catalogue; Film and Video Catalogue (on every aspect of natural history).

National Parks and Conservation Association
1015 31st St. N.W.
Washington, D.C. 20007
202-944-8530

Dedicated to defending, promoting, and improving America's national park system, the NPCA fulfills this mission by educating the public. Membership is $25 per year and includes the bimonthly magazine *National Parks*.

National Wildlife Federation
1400 16th St., N.W.
Washington, D.C. 20036-2266
202-797-6800

The NWF is a nonprofit conservation organization dedicated to creating and encouraging an awareness of the need for wise use of the Earth's resources among all the peoples of the world. It distributes a wide range of printed materials, sponsors outdoor education programs, and litigates environmental disputes in an effort to conserve natural resources and wildlife. Subscriptions to the monthly magazines *National Wildlife* and *International Wildlife* cost $15 per year; for *Ranger Rick*, a monthly magazine for children 6–12 years of age, $14 per year; and for *Big Backyard*, a monthly magazine for 3–5-year-olds, $10 per year. Educational materials: Backyard Wildlife Habitat Kit.

The Natural Guard
234 Shore Dr.
Guilford, CT 06437
203-457-0840

The Natural Guard offers children an opportunity to learn about the importance of environmental protection by exploring different environments and becoming involved in community action and chapter exchange projects.

Natural Resources Defense Council, Inc.
40 W. 20th St.
New York, NY 10011
212-727-2700

NRDC is committed to protecting America's endangered natural resources and improving the quality of the environment by bringing legal action, monitoring government agencies, and distributing information. Membership is $10 per year and includes the quarterly *Amicus Journal* and the bimonthly newsletter *Natural Resources Defense Council Newsline*.

The Nature Conservancy
1815 N. Lynn St.
Arlington, VA 22209
703-841-5300

The Nature Conservancy's mission is to identify and protect rare and endangered species by acquiring and preserving their habitats. Membership is $15 per year and includes the bimonthly *Nature Conservancy Magazine*, as well as state chapter newsletters.

Pacific Whale Foundation
101 N. Kihei Rd.
Kihei, HI 96753
800-942-5311

This group focuses on saving whales and the ocean environment. It provides public education programs and sponsors a Marine Debris Cleanup Day and a Whale Day. Membership is $25 for families, $20 for individuals, and $15 for students and seniors.

Rails to Trails Conservancy
1400 16th St., N.W., #300
Washington, D.C. 20036
202-797-5400

Rails to Trails actively engages in converting thousands of miles of abandoned railroad corridors into public trails for walking, bicycling, horseback riding, cross-country skiing, and for wildlife habitats. Membership is $18 per year.

Rainforest Action Network
301 Broadway, Suite A
San Francisco, CA 94133
415-398-4404

RAN focuses on rain forest protection. It works in tandem with other environmental and human rights organizations on important rain forest protection campaigns. Membership is $25 or $15 for those on a limited income. Two newsletters are included with membership: the monthly *Rain Forest Action Alert* and the quarterly *World Rain Forest Report*.

Rainforest Alliance
270 Lafayette St., Suite 512
New York, NY 10012
212-941-1900

The group's aim is to bring individuals and organizations together to help save rain forests. Memberships are $20 per year for individuals, and $15 per year for students and seniors, and include the quarterly newsletter *Canopy*.

Renew America
1400 16th St., N.W., Suite 710
Washington, D.C. 20036
202-232-2252

This organization, working at the federal, state, and private citizen level, provides an educational and networking forum devoted to the efficient use of natural resources. Membership is $25 per year and includes the quarterly *Renew America Report* and the yearly *State of States Report*.

Sierra Club
730 Polk St.
San Francisco, CA 94109
415-776-2211

Founded in 1892, the Sierra Club works to promote conservation of the natural environment by influencing public policy. Its more important campaigns include the Clean Air Act reauthorization; protection of the Arctic National Wildlife Refuge; national parks and forest protection; global warming/greenhouse effect; and international development lending reform. Membership is $33 per year and includes the monthly magazine *Sierra*.

Treepeople
12601 Mulholland Dr.
Beverly Hills, CA 90210
818-753-4600

This organization is dedicated to promoting personal involvement, community action, and global awareness of environmental issues. Activities include instructing citizens in tree-planting methods and maintenance, environmental leadership programs for children, and reforestation efforts in California. Membership is $25 per year and includes the bimonthly newsletter *Seedling News*.

Trees for Life
1103 Jefferson
Witchita, KS 67203
316-263-7294

Trees for Life provides funding, management, and expertise to people in developing countries for the cultivation of food (fruit- and vegetable-bearing trees) and fuel trees (species traditionally used for cooking and heating fuel). It also runs an education program for schoolchildren on the importance of trees.

The Trust for Public Land
116 New Montgomery
San Francisco, CA 94105
415-495-4014

The Trust for Public Land works to conserve land as a living resource for future and present generations. It has helped to establish over 150 local land trusts and preserve over half a million acres of public land.

Union of Concerned Scientists
26 Church St.
Cambridge, MA 02238
617-546-5552

This coalition of scientists, engineers, and other professionals conducts research on the problems of nuclear energy and weapons, and their effect on health, safety, environmental, and national security problems.

U.S. Public Interest Research Group
215 Pennsylvania Ave., S.E.
Washington, D.C. 20003
202-546-9707

Organized by Ralph Nader, USPIRG focuses on consumer and environmental protection, energy policy, and governmental and corporate reform. It monitors the implementation of Superfund and works for the legislation of clean air and pesticide safety bills. Membership is $25 per year and includes the quarterly *Citizen's Agenda*.

The Wilderness Society
1400 I St., N.W., 10th Fl.
Washington, D.C. 20005-2290
202-842-3400

The aim of the Wilderness Society is to protect wildlands, wildlife, forests, parks, rivers, and shorelands. The organization seeks to create an Arctic wildlife refuge, promote national park and eco-system management, and formulate a national forest policy. Membership, $15 the first year and $30 for each subsequent year, includes the bimonthly newsletter *The Wildlifer*.

Wildlife Information Center, Inc.
629 Green St.
Allentown, PA 18102
215-434-1637

Committed to securing and disseminating information on wildlife conservation and scientific research, this group's public education activities include in-service teacher training courses. Membership is $25 per year and includes the publication *Wildlife Activist*.

World Resources Institute
1709 New York Ave., N.W.
Washington, D.C. 20006
202-638-6800

This is a policy research center created to help governments, other organizations, and the private sector address the issues of environmental integrity, resource management, economic growth, and international security. It publishes the yearly *World Resources Report*.

World Wildlife Fund and The Conservation Foundation
1250 24th St., N.W.
Washington, D.C. 20037
202-293-4800

World Wildlife Fund and The Conservation Foundation (WWF) is the largest private U.S. organization workng worldwide to conserve nature. WWF works to preserve the diversity and abundance of life on Earth and the health of ecological systems by protecting natural areas and wildlife, promoting sustainable use of natural resources, and promoting more efficient resource and energy use and the maximum reduction of pollution. Membership is $15 per year and includes the bimonthly newsletter *Focus*, as well as periodic letters about upcoming projects.

Worldwatch Institute
1776 Massachusetts Ave., N.W.
Washington, D.C. 20036
202-452-1999

An independent research organization, the Worldwatch Institute alerts decision-makers and the general public to emerging global trends in the availability and management of resources. Its findings are published in various books and papers. Among its publications is the *State of the World* series. Membership is $20 per year and includes the bimonthly magazine *World Watch*.

BOOKS

As you probably know, the number of environmental books appearing in your local bookstores is growing all the time. Good! They are full of wonderful, thought-provoking, practical information. We suggest you take a look at a few of the following titles.

General Information
Listed in this section are some books that tackle the problems of the environment as a whole. Many critical issues are addressed in them, but one issue is not necessarily singled out as being more important than another. All of the titles provide tips and suggestions on ways that you, the reader, can contribute to saving the planet.

Design for a Livable Planet by John Naar. Harper & Row Publishers, 1990.

Embracing the Earth—Choices for Environmentally Sound Living by D. Mark Harris. The Noble Press Inc., 1990.

50 Simple Things You Can Do to Save the Earth by The Earthworks Group. Earthworks Press, 1989.

Hints for a Healthy Planet by Heloise. Putnam Publishing Group, 1990.

Our Common Future, The World Commission of Environment and Development. Oxford University Press, 1987.

Save Our Planet—750 Everyday Ways You Can Help Clean Up the Earth by Diane MacEachern. Dell Publishing, 1990.

2 Minutes for a Greener Planet by Marjorie Lamb. Harper & Row Publishers, 1990.

FOR KIDS
Earth Book for Kids—Activities to Help Heal the Environment by Linda Schwartz. The Learning Works, Inc., P.O. Box 6187, Santa Barbara, CA 93160, 1990.

Ecology—A Practical Introduction with Projects and Activities by Richard Spurgeon. EDC Publishing, 1988.

50 Simple Things Kids Can Do to Save the Earth by The Earthworks Group.

Going Green—A Handbook for Saving the Planet by John Elkington, Julia Hailes, Douglas Hill, and Joel Makower. Viking Press, 1990.

The Planet of Trash—An Environmental Fable by George Popple. National Press, Inc., 1989.

Environmental Issues

The books in the following sections address particular environmental issues. They offer suggestions on how you can help prevent further damage to the planet and how you can help in the "cleanup" process.

Air

Breathing Easier: Taking Action on Climate Change, Air Pollution, and Energy Insecurity by James J. MacKenzie. World Resources Institute, 1988.

The Healthy House by John Bower. Carol Communications, 1989.

The Nontoxic Home by Debra Lynn Dodd. St. Martin's Press, 1986.

Nontoxic & Natural by Debra Lynn Dodd. Jeremy P. Archer Inc., 1984.

Protecting the Ozone Layer: What You Can Do by Sarah J. Clark. Environmental Defense Fund, 1988.

Environmentally Responsible Products

Ecologue by Bruce Anderson. Prentice Hall Press, 1990.

Economics as if the Earth Really Mattered by Susan Meeker-Lowry. New Society Publisher, 1989.

The Green Consumer by John Elkington, Julia Hailes, and Joel Makower. Viking Penguin, 1990.

Shopping for a Better World: A Quick & Easy Guide to Socially Responsible Supermarket Shopping by the Council on Economic Priorities
P.O. Box 656
Big Bear Lake, CA 92315
714-584-1080 or 800-848-8876 (outside California)

NEWSLETTERS (PRODUCTS)

The Earthwise Consumer	The Green Consumer Letter
P.O. Box 1506	1526 Connecticut Ave., N.W.
Mill Valley, CA 94942	Washington, D.C. 20036
415-383-5892	202-332-1700
$20/year, eight issues	$27/year, twelve issues

Flora and Fauna

Extinction: The Causes and Consequences of the Disappearance of Species by Paul Ehrlich and Anne Ehrlich. Ballantine, 1983.
The Man Who Planted Hope and Grew Happiness by Jean Giono. Friends of Nature, 1967.
The Sense of Wonder by Rachel Carson. Harper and Row, 1956.
State of the Ark by Lee Durrell. Doubleday, 1986.

FOR KIDS

Discovering Endangered Species by Nancy Field and Sally Machlis. Dog-Eared Publications, 1990.
The Lorax by Dr. Seuss. Random House, 1971.

Food

Diet for a New America by John Robbins. Stillpoint Publishing, 1987.
Diet for a Small Planet by Francis Moore Lappe. Ballantine Books, 1982.

Outdoor Education

Hug a Tree—And Other Things to Do Outdoors with Young Children by Robert E. Rockwell, Elizabeth A. Sherwood, and Robert A. Williams. Gryphon House, Inc., 1983.

The Kids Nature Book—365 Indoor/Outdoor Activities by Susan Milord. Williamson Publishing, Church Hill Rd., Charlotte, VT 05445, 1989.
The Nature Book by Midas Dekkers. Macmillan Publishing Company, 1988.
Sharing the Joy of Nature—Nature Activities for All Ages by Joseph Cornell. Dawn Publications, 1989.
Sharing Nature with Children—A Parents' and Teachers' Nature Awareness Guidebook by Joseph Bharat Cornell. Ananda Publications, 1979.

The Rain Forest
Lessons of the Rainforest by Suzanne Head and Robert Heinzman. Sierra Club Books, 1990.
Race to Save the Tropics, edited by Robert Goodland. Island Press, 1990.
The Rainforest Book by Scott Lewis, with the Natural Resources Defense Council. Living Planet Press, 1990.

FOR KIDS
Color the Rainforest. Living Planet Press, 1990.
The Great Kapok Tree by Lynne Cherry. Gulliver Books, Harcourt Brace Jovanovich, 1990.
The Tropical Rainforest by Jeanne Craighead George. Crowell, 1990.

Recycling
Complete Trash—The Best Way to Get Rid of Everything Around the House by Norm Crampton. M. Evans and Company, Inc., 1990.
Planning for Community Recycling: A Citizen's Guide to Resources. Environmental Action, 1525 New Hampshire Ave., N.W., Washington, D.C. 20036, 1990.
Recycling Works! State and Local Solutions to Solid Waste Management Problems. EPA Office of Solid Waste, 401 M St., S.W., Washington, D.C. 20460, 1989.
War on Waste—Can America Win Its Battle with Garbage? by Louis Blumberg and Robert Gottlieb. Island Press, 1989.

FOR KIDS
Here Today, Here Tomorrow. New Jersey Department of Environmental Protection, 1989. (A teacher's guide on solid-waste management for schoolchildren grades 4–8, but applicable for family use.) *The Planet of Trash: An Environmental Fable* by George Poppel. National Press, Inc., 1987.

Travel

Directory of Alternative Travel Resources by Dianne Brause, 1988. *Directory of Environmental Travel Resources* by Dianne Brause, forthcoming.

Both available from:

One World Family Travel Network
Lost Valley Center
81868 Lost Valley Lane
Dexter, OR 97431
503-937-3351

Water

The Forest of the Sea by John L. Culliny. Sierra Club Books, 1976.
The Wasted Ocean: The Ominous Crisis of Marine Pollution and How to Stop It by David R. Bulloch. Lyons and Burford, 1989.
The Water Planet by Lyall Watson. Crown Publishing, Random House, 1988.

FOR KIDS
The Ocean Book by the Center for Environmental Education. John Wiley & Sons, 1989.

MAGAZINES AND PERIODICALS

AUDUBON ACTIVIST
National Audubon Society
950 Third Ave.
New York, NY 10022
212-832-3200
$9/year, six issues

BUZZWORM
Buzzworm, Inc.
1818 16th St.
Boulder, CO 80302
$18/year, six issues
303-442-1969

E MAGAZINE
28 Knight St.
Norwalk, Ct 06851
800-825-0061
$20/year, six issues

ENDANGERED SPECIES
UPDATE
School of Natural Resources
The University of Michigan
Ann Arbor, MI 48109-1115
$23/year, ten issues; $18/year
for students and senior citizens

GARBAGE—THE PRACTICAL
JOURNAL FOR THE ENVI-
RONMENT
Old House Journal Corp.
435 Ninth St.
Brooklyn, NY 11215
718-788-1700
$21/year, six issues
800-888-9070

HARROWSMITH
Ferry Rd.
Charlotte, VT 05445
802-425-3961
$21/year, six issues
800-344-3350

ORGANIC GARDENING
MAGAZINE
Rodale Press, Inc.
33 E. Minor St.
Emmaus, PA 18098
$18/year, ten issues
215-967-5171

RECYCLING TODAY
G.I.E. Publishers, Inc.
4012 Bridge Ave.
Cleveland, OH 44113
216-961-4130
$32/year, twelve issues
800-456-0707

RESOURCE RECYCLING
North America's Recycling
   Journal
P.O. Box 10540
Portland, OR 97210
503-227-1319 or
   800-227-1424
$42/year, twelve issues

FOR KIDS

P3: THE EARTH-BASED MAGAZINE FOR KIDS
P3 Foundation
P.O. Box 52
Montgomery, VT 05470
$14/year, ten issues

RANGER RICK
National Wildlife Federation
1400 16th St., N.W.
Washington, D.C. 20036-2266
$14/year, twelve issues

WORLD
National Geographic Society
P.O. Box 2330
Washington, D.C. 20077-9955
$12.95/year, twelve issues

COMPUTER NETWORKS

Up-to-date environmental information is now available through your office or home computer. The following companies provide "on-line" services to help you gather and share valuable environmental information.

EarthNet
P.O. Box 330072
Kahului, Maui, HI 96733
808-872-6090

EarthNet describes itself as a "prototype interactive global culture, an abundant ecology of shared ideas and experiences." Available on-line services include *EarthNet News and Info, Village Resource Center,* and *Village Bazaar.*

EcoNet
18 deDoom St.
San Francisco, CA 94107
415-442-0220

EcoNet is a full-service international environmental telecommunications network. It features E-mail, teleconferencing, database, fax, and telex services. It has fully integrated connections with partner networks in several countries.

EnviroNet
Greenpeace Action
139 Townsend, 4th Fl.
San Francisco, CA 94107
415-512-9025

Greenpeace Action sponsors this network, which is open to the public free of charge. It features E-mail and conferencing on topics such as energy, deforestation, and toxins.

Kids Network
National Geographic Society
Educational Services
Department 1001
Washington, D.C. 20077
800-368-2728

Sponsored by the National Geographic Society, this is a tele-communications-based science and geography curriculum. Students from all over North America are linked via electronic mail.

HOTLINES

For information and updates on pending environmental legislation and suggestions on who to write:

Audubon Hotline
202-547-9017 or 202-547-9009

For information or concern about the condition of your drinking water:

EPA Safe Drinking Water Hotline
800-426-4791

To report animal poaching incidents in our national parks:

National Parks and Conservation Association Hotline
800-448-NPCA (6722)

To report the release of oil and other hazardous substances into the environment:

National Response Center
800-424-8802

GLOSSARY

Acid Rain—The mixture of sulphur dioxide, nitrogen oxide, and water falling as rain (or snow). It can destroy wildlife and marine life, crops, trees, and buildings.

Aquifers—The underground stores of water that replenish water systems.

Atmosphere—The layer of gases (mostly nitrogen and oxygen) about 310 miles thick that surrounds the Earth and protects us from the sun's harmful ultraviolet rays.

Biodegradable—The property of a substance that allows it to be broken down by microorganisms.

Chlorofluorocarbons (CFCs)—Chlorine-based compounds that are used in aerosols, refrigerators, and polystyrene (such as Styrofoam) and which contribute to the destruction of the ozone layer.

Compost—The layering of organic waste, usually food scraps, lawn clippings, and fallen leaves, so that decomposition will occur and result in a fertile humus used to enrich garden soils.

Coniferous—The type of trees whose leaves remain green throughout the seasons (also called evergreens).

Conservation—To conserve something means to "save" it. We only have one planet, and in order to keep it safe and healthy for future generations, we must practice the conservation of our air, water, soil, animals, plants, and minerals.

Deciduous—The type of trees whose leaves die and fall from the branches.

Decompose—To breakdown into organic components.

Deforestation—The disappearance of all the trees from a particular area. It can occur naturally when a fire sweeps through a forest, or when a flood washes all the trees away. It can also be caused by the human activity of developing an area or clearing it for agricultural purposes.

Diversity—The biological differences between all living things, as in "biodiversity."

Drought—A prolonged period of dryness.

Ecosystem—A natural system—such as a forest, coral reef, or desert—made up of living parts (animals, birds, plants, etc.) and nonliving parts (rocks, water, soil, etc.), all working together and depending on one another for survival.

Endangered Species—A plant or animal species that is threatened with extinction.

Energy—The basic force that allows all living things to function.

Environment—All the living and nonliving components that surround and affect an organism.

Erosion—The wearing away of the Earth's soil by the overgrazing of animals, deforestation, glacier activity, water movement, or wind.

Extinction—The complete disappearance of a species.

Food Chain—The cycle that links plants and animals together. Picture it as a pyramid with ascending layers of increasingly complex life forms. On top are humans and large animals. On the bottom are simple plants such as plankton (found in the sea). The plankton are eaten by invertebrates, the organisms above them in the chain. Invertebrates, in turn, are eaten by fish. Fish are eaten by seabirds; seabirds are eaten by large marine mammals. There are many such food chains, each having the same sort of structure, but only human beings have the capacity to destroy the entire chain through environmental destruction.

Food Cooperatives—Stores owned and operated by their patrons and usually selling unpackaged organic foods in bulk.

Fossil Fuels—Coal, oil, and natural gas. These fuels are formed in the Earth from the remains of plants and animals.

Global Warming—see Greenhouse Effect.

Green—This is not just a word used to define a particular color. It is also becoming the word used to symbolize the environmental movement—its practices, products, and politics.

Greenhouse Effect—The trapping of solar heat within the Earth's atmosphere as a result of the buildup of heat-absorbing gases such as carbon dioxide, resulting in a rise in the Earth's temperature (also known as "global warming").

Groundwater—Water found between the spaces in rock and soil particles under the soil.

Habitat—The native environment of a particular plant or animal.

Hazardous Waste—The waste left over from the production process when a product such as plastic is manufactured. Manufacturing wastes are often poisonous, or hazardous.

Landfill—A dumping site for solid waste.

Leachate—The liquid waste from a landfill.

Methane—A gas that is the by-product of organic decomposition.

Mulch—A protective covering of leaves, compost, paper, etc., used to prevent soil erosion, enrich the soil, and control weeds.

Nature—Everything not man-made: trees, water, soil, sky, plants, animals, birds, insects, wind, rain, and so on.

Organic—Anything that is or was part of an organism and contains the element carbon.

Ozone Layer—The upper layer of the Earth's atmosphere containing the ozone gas that prohibits the sun's harmful rays from penetrating the atmosphere.

Pesticides—Chemicals used to kill weeds and insects that may damage crops.

Phosphates—A salt or a fragrant compound of phosphoric acid.

Pollution—The contamination of an area with toxic substances or an excess of natural substances, such as the infiltration of salt water into fresh water.

Radon—A radioactive gas formed when radium disintegrates.

Rain Forests—Forests that grow in tropical areas near the equator where it is very hot and rain falls daily.

Recycling—Reusing materials rather than disposing of them.

Smog—Pollution from cars and factories that mixes with the air and forms visible layers of dirty air.

Solid Waste—The semi-solid and solid forms of waste material, including garbage (food waste), household trash, industrial waste, construction waste, ash, and yard waste.

Species—A population of similar organisms that can interbreed.

Toxicity—The poisonous quality of manufactured products such as pesticides or waste products such as ash.

RECYCLING RESOURCES

Contact the state government offices and private organizations listed below for further information regarding recycling efforts in your state. They can tell you about schedules for pickup, independent recyclers you can deliver to, methods for recycling certain toxins, etc.

alabama
Department of Environmental Management
Solid Waste Branch, Land Division
17151 Congressman Dickinson Dr.
Montgomery, AL 36130
205-271-7700

alaska
Department of Environmental Conservation, Recycling
P.O. Box O
Juneau, AK 99811-1800
907-465-2671

arizona
Department of Environmental Quality
Waste Planning Section, 4th Fl.
205 N. Central
Phoenix, AZ 85004
602-257-7444

arkansas
Pollution Control and Ecology
Solid Waste Management Division
8001 National Dr.
Little Rock, AR 72219
501-562-7444

california
Department of Conservation
Division of Recycling
1025 P St.
Sacramento, CA 95814
916-323-3743 or 800-322-SAVE (7283), for the recycling center nearest you.

California Resource Recovery Association
13223 Black Mountain Rd., I-300
San Diego, CA 92129

Integrated Waste Management
1020 Ninth St., Suite 300
Sacramento, CA 95814
916-322-3330

colorado
Department of Health
Hazardous Materials and Waste Management Division
4210 E. 11th Ave., Room 351
Denver, CO 80220
303-331-4830

connecticut
Department of Recycling
State Office Building
165 Capitol Ave.
Hartford, CT 06106
203-566-8722

Connecticut Recyclers Coalition
P.O. Box 445
Stonington, CT 06378

delaware
Department of Natural Resources
and Environmental Control
Division of Air and Waste Management
P.O. Box 1401
89 Kings Hwy.
Dover, DE 19903
302-739-3820

district of columbia
Office of Recycling
65 K St., Lower Level
Washington, D.C. 20002
202-939-7116

florida
Department of Environmental
Regulation
Division of Waste Management
2600 Blairstone Rd.
Tallahassee, FL 32399
904-488-0300

Recycle Florida
c/o Department of Environmental
Regulation
Solid Waste Division
(address same as above)

georgia
Department of Natural Resources
Environmental Protection Division
3420 Norman Berry Dr., 7th Fl.
Hapeville, GA 30305
404-656-2836

Department of Community Affairs
1200 Equitable Building
100 Peachtree St.
Atlanta, GA 30303
404-656-3898

hawaii
Department of Health
Solid and Hazardous Waste Division
5 Waterfront Plaza, Suite 250
500 Ala-Moana Blvd.
Honolulu, HI 96813
808-543-8227

Recycling Association of Hawaii
162-B North King St.
Honolulu, HI 96817
808-599-1976

idaho
Division of Environmental Quality
IWRAP Bureau, Hazardous Materials Branch
1410 N. Hilton
Boise, ID 83706
208-334-5879

illinois
Office of Solid Waste and Renewable Resources
325 W. Adams
Springfield, IL 62704-1892
217-524-5454

Illinois Recycling Association
407 S. Dearborn, #1775
Chicago, IL 60637
312-939-2985

indiana
Department of Environmental
Management
Office of Solid and Hazardous
Waste Management
105 S. Meridian St.
Indianapolis, IN 46225
317-232-8883

Indiana Recycling Coalition
P.O. Box 6357
Lafayette, IN 47903

iowa
Department of Natural Resources
Waste Management Authority Division
900 E. Grand Ave.
Des Moines, IA 50319
515-281-4968

Iowa Recycling Association
P.O. Box 3184
Des Moines, IA 50316

kansas
Department of Health and Environment
Department of Solid Waste Management
Building 740, Forbes Field
Topeka, KS 66620
913-296-1590

kentucky
Division of Waste Management
Resource Recovery Branch
18 Reilly Rd.
Frankfort, KY 40601
502-564-6716

Kentucky Recycling Association
c/o Urban County Government
Department of Public Works
200 E. Main
Lexington, KY 40507

louisiana
Department of Environmental
 Quality
P.O. Box 44096
Baton Rouge, LA 70804-4096
504-342-9103

maine
Waste Management Agency
State House Station #154
Augusta, ME 04333
207-289-5300

Maine Resource and Recovery Association
c/o Maine Municipal Association
Community Dr.
Augusta, ME 04330

maryland
Department of Environmental
 Quality
Hazardous Waste Program
2500 Broening Hwy., Bldg. 40, 2nd
 Fl.
Baltimore, MD 21224
301-631-3343

Maryland Recycling Coalition
101 Monroe, 6th Fl.
Rockville, MD 20850

massachusetts
Department of Environmental Protection
Division of Solid Waste Management
1 Winter St., 4th Fl.
Boston, MA 02108
617-292-5980

MassRecycle
P.O. Box 3111
Worcester, MA 01613

michigan
Department of Natural Resources
Waste Management Division
P.O. Box 30241
Lansing, MI 48909
517-373-2730

Michigan Recycling Coalition
P.O. Box 10240
Lansing, MI 48901

minnesota
Office of Waste Management
1350 Energy Lane, Suite 201
St. Paul, MN 55108
612-649-5750

Recycling Association of Minnesota
c/o The Minnesota Project
2222 Elm St., S.E.
Minneapolis, MN 55414

mississippi
Department of Environmental Quality
Office of Pollution Control
P.O. Box 10385
Jackson, MS 39289-0385
601-961-5171

missouri
Department of Natural Resources
P.O. Box 176
Jefferson City, MO 65102
314-751-3176

Missouri State Recycling Association
P.O. Box 331
St. Charles, MO 63301

montana
Department of Health and Environmental Science
Solid and Hazardous Waste Bureau
Cogswell Building
Helena, MT 59620
406-444-2821

Associated Recyclers of Montana
458 Charles
Billings, MT 59101

Keep Montana Clean and Beautiful
P.O. Box 5925
2021 11th Ave.
Helena, MT 59601

nebraska
Department of Environmental Control
Litter Reduction and Recycling Program
P.O. Box 98922
State House Station
Lincoln, NE 68509-8922
402-471-2186

Nebraska State Recycling Association
P.O. Box 80729
Lincoln, NE 68501

nevada
Office of Community Services
Energy Extension Service
Capitol Complex
Carson City, NV 89710
702-687-4908

Nevada Recycling Coalition
2550 Thomas Jefferson
Reno, NV 89509

new hampshire
Environmental Services Department
Waste Management Division
6 Hazen Dr.
Concord, NH 03301-6509
603-271-2926

New Hampshire Resource Recovery Association
P.O. Box 721
Concord, NH 03301-0721

new jersey
Department of Environmental Protection
Office of Recycling
850 Bear Tavern Rd.
Trenton, NJ 08625-0414
609-530-4001

Association of New Jersey Recyclers
120 Finderne
Bridgewater, NJ 08807

new mexico
Environmental Improvement Division
Solid Waste Bureau
Harold Runnels Bldg.
1190 St. Francis Dr.
Santa Fe, NM 87503
505-827-2959

Recycle New Mexico
c/o Office of Recycling
P.O. Box 1293
Albuquerque, NM 87103

new york
Department of Environmental Conservation
Waste Reduction and Recycling
50 Wolf Rd.
Albany, NY 12233-4015
518-457-7337

north carolina
Solid Waste Section
P.O. Box 27687
Raleigh, NC 27611-7687
919-733-0692

north dakota
Department of Health
Division of Waste Management
P.O. Box 5520
Bismarck, ND 58502-5520
701-224-2366

ohio
Litter Prevention and Recycling
Department of Natural Resources
1889 Fountain Square, Bldg. F-2
Columbus, OH 43224
614-265-6353

oklahoma
Department of Health
Solid Waste Services
P.O. Box 53551
Oklahoma City, OK 73152
405-271-7169

oregon
Department of Environmental Quality
Waste Reduction Section
811 S.W. Sixth Ave., 8th Fl.
Portland, OR 97204
503-229-5913

pennsylvania
Department of Environmental Resources
Bureau of Waste Management, Waste Reduction/Recycling
P.O. Box 2063
Harrisburg, PA 17105-2063
717-787-7382

rhode island
Department of Environmental Management
O.S.C.A.R.
83 Park St., 5th Fl.
Providence, RI 02903
401-277-3434

south carolina
Bureau of Solid and Hazardous Waste
2600 Bull St.
Columbia, SC 29201
803-732-5200

south dakota
Department of Water and Natural Resources
Waste Management Program
523 E. Capitol St.
Pierre, SD 57501
605-773-3153

tennessee
Department of Health and Environment
Solid Waste Management Division
701 Broadway, 4th Fl.
Customs House
Nashville, TN 37247-3520
615-741-3424

texas
Department of Health
Division of Solid Waste Management
1100 W. 49th St.
Austin, TX 78756
512-458-7271

utah
Department of Environmental Health
Solid and Hazardous Waste
P.O. Box 16690
Salt Lake City, UT 84116-0690
801-538-6170

vermont
Department of Environmental Conservation
Solid Waste Division
103 S. Main St., West Bldg.
Waterbury, VT 05676
802-244-7831

virginia
Department of Waste Management
The Monroe Bldg., 11th Fl.
101 N. 14th St.
Richmond, VA 23219
703-225-2667 or 800-522-2075

washington
Department of Ecology
Recycling Information Office
Elkenberry Building
4407 Woodview Dr., S.E.
Lacey, WA 98503
206-459-6731 or 800-RECYCLE
(732-9253)

west virginia
Division of Natural Resources
Solid Waste Section
1356 Hansford St.
Charleston, WV 25301
304-348-5993

wisconsin
Department of Natural Resources
Bureau of Solid and Hazardous Waste Management
P.O. Box 7921
Madison, WI 53707
608-267-7566

wyoming
Department of Environmental Quality
Solid Waste Management
122 W. 25th St.
Herschler Building, 4th Fl., W.
Cheyenne, WY 82002
307-777-7752

EFFECTIVE LETTER WRITING

Voicing an opinion in this country is one of the most cherished rights of its citizens. Often the ears we need to reach are not as accessible as we would like them to be, but there are ways of reaching them. By far one of the best and most personal is through a letter-writing campaign. These letters can be used to address an environmental or social issue of concern to you and can be written to company CEOs, to your congressmen and senators, and to the President himself.

Know the environmental voting record of your elected officials. Write letters to these representatives in support of their actions. Encourage a larger environmental policy agenda in order to enlighten the public about the value of our land.

An effective letter has a number of important components you should be aware of.

▶ **1** For letters addressed to political representatives, you must carefully *identify the issue and any potential legislation that may be connected with it.* Legislation already introduced will have a bill number, and it should be used if you know it. You can find this information by contacting:

The U.S. Government Printing Office
941 N. Capitol St.
Washington, D.C. 20401
202-783-3238

▶ **2** Write to your own representative and to the members of the committee responsible for legislating the issue that concerns you.
▶ **3** In the address portion of your letter use the proper title of the person to whom you are writing. Both congressmen and senators are generally referred to as "The Honorable" when you are using their title, and you may use "Dear Senator _____," "Dear Congressman(woman) _____," or "Dear Mr./Mrs. _____" in the salutation. In any event, be courteous. The staff members who open

the mail are much more likely to see that your letter reaches the right person if it is polite and nonaggressive.

▶ **4** Be brief. State your concerns and your opinion about proposed legislation on a particular issue, or the need for legislation if none has yet been proposed, in as concise a manner as possible. The ideal letter is seldom longer than one page.

▶ **5** For address information, or to pass your views along via the telephone, call: the President at 202-456-1414; the U.S. Senate at 202-224-3121; and the U.S. House of Representatives at 202-456-1414.

▶ **6** Encourage others to write as well. There is strength in numbers. Make it a community activity—a joint office project, a PTA project. The more people who speak out in unison, the louder your message will be.

▶ **7** Encourage children to participate in a letter-writing campaign. Their concerns are just as worthy of consideration. After all, they are the future voters of this country.

▶ **8** Encourage children to write their own letters to companies when a particular product fails them. This will almost always be a toy, a child's primary consumer item, so let them express their dissatisfaction at the way a toy is manufactured, or packaged, etc. It is excellent preparation for their emerging skills as responsible consumers.

▶ **9** Make letter writing a school project. Again, a joint effort creates a "louder" voice. Children can share ideas and thoughts they would like to express. An infusion of many ideas makes for a first-rate letter.

▶ **10** Keep copies of all letters (preferably on a home computer) so that they can be used again if necessary. If you keep them on a computer, you can simply change the address and salutation without having to retype the whole letter. It will also allow you to gauge the response time of the recipient and when it may be appropriate to send a second copy of the letter or a new one.